Towards an
Australian Architecture

Towards an
Australian Architecture

Edited and photographed by Harry Sowden

Lund Humphries, London

First published in the
United Kingdom in 1970 by
Lund Humphries Publishers Limited
12 Bedford Square London WC1
First published in Australia
by Ure Smith Sydney
a division of Horwitz Group Books
2 Denison Street
North Sydney NSW 2060

SBN 85331 262 1

Designed and produced in Australia
Printed in Hong Kong by
Dai Nippon Printing Company
(International) Ltd

Designed by Harry Sowden

Acknowledgments
The Editor would like to thank the
following for their help in the
preparation of this book: Donald
Gazzard, architect, Glenn Murcutt,
architect, and Irene Smith,
typographer. All the photographs in
the book were taken with Mamiya
camera equipment

The photograph on the front of the
jacket shows the main building in
Australia Square, Sydney, and the
one on the back of the jacket shows
the Royal Insurance Group Building,
Melbourne

Contents

Contents (continued)

Contents (continued)

Preface

Very little is known of Australia's architecture outside its capital cities and, even there, it suffers from lack of appreciation or involvement. Australia is a large continent with small scale thinking in architectural development, and the architect's place in its growing community has yet to be recognized. It is a country that relies on the standard image of the typical Australian with his gambling instincts to pay by lotteries for its finest example of twentieth century building, the Sydney Opera House. Yet political intrigue brings about the architect's resignation and allows his vision to be turned into something fit for musical comedy.

Books have been written to point out the shortcomings of architecture and man-made environment in Australia. But what about the minority of architects who do care, and whose work stands out like islands in this sea of ugliness? These are the men who are turning their backs on styles that have been copied from magazines in an attempt to overcome the geographical isolation of Australia, and who are rejecting the tomato ketchup embellishment that has been in vogue for the last thirty years.

In this book I wish to give some of these architects who are working towards a new identity the opportunity to communicate. It would, of course, be impossible to include all the better work being done, but it is an attempt to show a selection of the many faces of architecture; to create an awareness and greater understanding of architecture in Australia. For, until this happens, our environment is unlikely to improve.

Harry Sowden

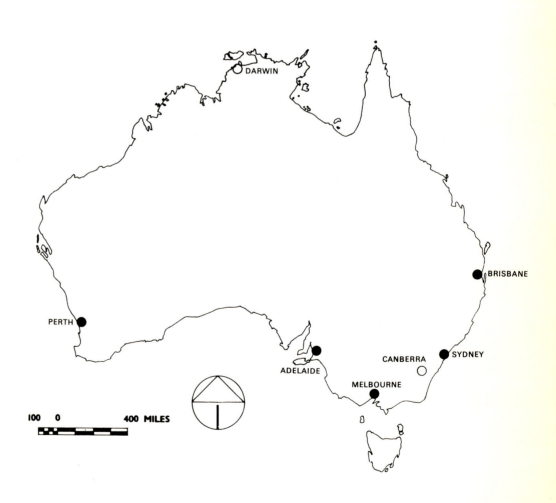

DARWIN

PERTH

BRISBANE

ADELAIDE

CANBERRA

SYDNEY

MELBOURNE

100 0 400 MILES

Introduction

The short story of architecture in Australia in the 180 years since the first European settlement was started on the site of the present city of Sydney can be conveniently divided into three epochs of diminishing length.

Each of these epochs was heralded by the arrival (and almost as quick departure) of Hero-Architects who set down certain standards and refused to compromise. Like all heroes, conscious of their role, they were difficult people. They coincided with significant periods of Australian history and aspirations.

The first Hero-Architect, Francis Greenway, arrived in Sydney involuntarily twenty-six years after the founding of the convict settlement. Greenway was born in 1777 and after training as an architect in London, practised in Bristol and Bath. In 1812 he was convicted of forging part of a contract and, as this was a capital offence, was sentenced to death. Through the petitioning of friends, his sentence was commuted to fourteen years transportation, and he subsequently arrived in Sydney in February 1814 with a letter of recommendation to the Governor, Lachlan Macquarie. Macquarie himself had arrived only four years earlier and, unlike his predecessors, had visions of transforming the infant colony. One of his first requests had been for an architect to be sent out 'with ideas, taste and a drawing board complete'.

Although the records are hazy, Greenway must have established himself fairly quickly as an architect for, by 1816, Macquarie had appointed him Government Architect at a salary of three shillings a day. In the ensuing five years, Morton Herman, the architectural historian, records[1] that his work included a lighthouse, two barracks, a fort, a magazine, three churches, three houses, two courthouses, a large block of stables, a large school, a large reformatory, a fountain, an obelisk, a toll gate, a large stores building, a dyke, a market house, a hospital, a military mess house, a police office, and a quay; as well as making major alterations to ten buildings and a dockyard. In addition he began projects for a cathedral, town sewers, a water supply, fortifications, and bridges. With his artistic temperament, quick temper and strong integrity, he made many enemies as he attempted to introduce better materials and workmanship into slipshod and corrupt building practice. He started compiling draft building laws, training workmen and innovating new contractual procedures. This body of work would be an achievement at any time but was even more so as Greenway, with no clerical or drafting assistance, did all the supervision himself, often at considerable distances. Yet he was a moody and difficult person and there was an inevitable air about his final quarrel with Macquarie, who had been his patron and protector.

Macquarie was recalled to England for extravagance, and Greenway was dismissed shortly afterwards to disappear into obscurity.

Macquarie, it has been said, had found, on his arrival, a gaol, but left a colony, and Greenway had made the most of the opportunities given him before he finally went too far and fell into disfavour. Our first Hero-Architect had set architectural standards of a high order, had involved himself with improving the technique of building and, with strong integrity and consciousness of his self-appointed role, had introduced professional standards of estimating, progress payments and other ways of protecting his clients' interests. The years that followed showed the gradual decline of the ideas and the standards adopted by Francis Greenway. Mortimer Lewis and John Verge were honourable successors but, except for a brief flowering in Tasmania (John Lee Archer and James Blackburn), Georgian influence had waned and passed before the other colonies developed. The 1830s saw the beginning of stylistic eclecticism, the Gothic revival flowered briefly with Edmund Blackett, and Greenway was forgotten. Architectural decline was fortunately not matched in other ways. The ensuing years were ones of great political, social and economic change. Three new experimental free settlements in Western Australia, South Australia and Port Phillip (now Melbourne) — pastoral offshoots of the convict colonies — were founded. Population increased rapidly, and by 1840, when the transportation of convicts ceased, there were more than 400,000 people in the colonies, over half of whom were free immigrants from Great Britain.

Even in those early days Australia was one of the most urbanized countries in the world, with a very high proportion of the population living in two or three cities. Then, with the discovery of gold in NSW and Victoria, the influx of people rushing to the goldfields trebled the population within ten years to 1,170,000. Colonial society suddenly became much more complex with the enormous, quick wealth that came from the goldfields.

The affluence of this post gold rush era led to a Victorian architecture of an extravagance unequalled anywhere in the world, with cast iron balustrades and decorative features that came to be known as 'iron lace'.

The inner areas of Sydney and Melbourne rapidly expanded at this time as the Victorian terraced house suburbs of Paddington and Carlton were built by speculators. These were to decline into slums as the cities moved outwards but were rescued after the Second World War to become the smart Chelseas of their respective cities. Owing to their simplicity as townhouses and their picturesque suitability for a hilly terrain they remain as a high point of Victorian architecture.

Out in the country, however, there were fewer self-conscious architectural pretensions than in the 'Boom' style buildings of the cities. An Australian vernacular tradition of building had grown up largely using corrugated

St Matthew's, Francis Greenway

Victorian terraced houses

galvanized iron sheeting, a mid century invention destined to become the great Australian building material. These simple country farmhouses, wool sheds, saw mills and wheat silos had evolved in their design buildings that have an immediately recognizable Australian quality—a quality gained through their simplicity and straightforward functional attitudes and their healthy respect for the climate.

Australian architectural development declined for the remainder of the nineteenth century. In 1913, after winning an international competition for the design of the new national capital, Canberra, the second Hero-Architect, Walter Burley Griffin, arrived in Australia.

Griffin came from Chicago, which had been a city of architectural invention and ferment in the thirty years before the Canberra competition. Under the leadership of Louis Sullivan, the ideas of the Chicago school were to influence the rest of the world, and Griffin, as a young man, participated in this development. He was a contemporary of Frank Lloyd Wright and had worked with him during the period of the prairie houses. He brought to provincial Australia a consciousness of the most creative architectural ideas of the outside world coupled with a strong will and integrity.

During the war years, Griffin developed the design of the new capital and supervised construction until 1920 when his contract was not renewed by the Government. He suffered continual bureaucratic obstruction and very little of the city as planned was built until after the Second World War, when he

was revealed as a site planner of great skill and vision. His interest in landscape architecture and town planning —his concern for a total environment, and not just architecture in a narrow sense—was years ahead of his time.

After the whole sorry mess of lies and intrigue of the Canberra episode Griffin moved to Melbourne, where his major buildings in Australia, the Capitol Theatre and Newman College, were built. These were fine assured buildings in any company, although the Capitol Theatre has since been demolished. Before he finally left Australia in 1936, Griffin developed a Sydney harbourside suburb called Castlecrag, planned the two new towns of Leeton and Griffith, and built a small number of houses in Sydney and Melbourne. Although he was a difficult, unreliable man in many ways he was quite practical. He patented a window stay at the time of the Canberra competition and later developed a concrete block construction system, yet his buildings were often badly detailed and constructed due to innovations not followed through.

This period spanned a world-wide economic depression and was a hard time for a sensitive architect who was not given enough opportunity to develop his talent. Yet for all his faults, his work, his environmentalist ideals and his uncompromising integrity stood out as a unique example for Australian architects to emulate. His influence unfortunately was slight and it has been left to a later generation to rediscover him[2]. Except for individualists like Harold Desbrowe Annear, an Australian contemporary of Griffin, who went his own way and died in 1933, Australian architecture crawled on its pedestrian path, and Griffin's example was ignored.

The stage of Australian history that began with a wave of optimism and nationalist feeling at the beginning of the century, and threw up Griffin as its architectural conscience, gradually bumbled its weary way to a conclusion with the Second World War.

The economic effects of wartime isolation which forced the development of Australian industries and technology, and the political effects of the war in the Pacific which increased Australia's dependence on the United States, set the scene for the third period of the country's development.

With assisted migration from Europe, until one in every six people was a New Australian, the population steadily grew. The architectural scene was being agitated at this time by a small group of architects who had been influenced by Griffin, and by events overseas. Roy Grounds in Melbourne and Sydney Ancher in Sydney, who had returned to Australia in the mid-thirties after years abroad, began building houses that aroused the enthusiasm of their students and shocked local Councils.

Robin Boyd, an architect with a genius for coining words such as 'featurism' that have since passed into our language, began his career at this time, and became the architectural conscience of the Australian scene with his book *The Australian Ugliness*[3].

Another impetus was given by the arrival in 1948 of Harry Seidler, who had been taught at Harvard by the founder of the Bauhaus, Walter Gropius. Seidler set about imparting the message of the one true architecture with a zeal and integrity which he still maintains. He quickly learnt respect for the Sydney sun and has few equals in Australia for the vigorous rationality of his approach to architecture[4].

None of these men managed to provide real leadership for a generation growing up after the war, although they influenced many people. With their buildings, however, they undoubtedly started to create the conditions and set the scene for the arrival of the third Hero-Architect.

In 1955 the international competition for the Sydney Opera House was announced, the two eminent architects, Eero Saarinen and Sir Leslie Martin, being part of the jury. With a post war affluence second only to North America, Sydney was determined with enthusiasm to show the rest of the world.

The result was announced in January 1957. With 234 designs submitted from 30 countries the winner was a relatively unknown Dane, Joern Utzon. Utzon had won a few competitions in Denmark and built some interesting houses and groups of houses, but his name was known outside Denmark at that time only to those who diligently scanned overseas architectural journals.

His design was acclaimed enthusiastically. For political reasons construction commenced within two years,

Country farmhouse

Suburbia

prematurely, as it happened, because the structural problems associated with the soaring shell roofs had not been solved. The original free form of the shells had to be changed. A brilliant modification, basing the form of the shells on segments of the surface of a sphere, enabled them to be precast in identical concrete segments.

The project by this time had aroused world-wide architectural enthusiasm. Siegfried Giedion, the historian and architectural propagandist, added to his bible of the modern movement in architecture *Space Time and Architecture* a chapter devoted to 'Utzon and the Sydney Opera House'.

The final chapter of this story is well known and yet we are too close for it to be told well. History seems to be repeating itself. Like the other hero-architects, Utzon was too demanding with his perfectionist attitudes for a still small and provincial society, where near enough is often good enough. In a situation which is not black and white the greater fault is clearly with the society who failed to understand, absorb and guide him, and with an establishment who had clearly learnt nothing from the history of Walter Burley Griffin.

Egalitarian and populist ideas are still so strong in Australia that there is a tendency when someone wants to criticize anything Australian to blame the society, the people, anything but the group directly concerned.

Australian architecture has been dull, not just because Australian society has been so provincial, but because Australian architects have not been good enough.

The question to be asked is whether the generation that follows the Sydney Opera House will succeed in bringing Australia into the ranks of those countries to be taken seriously in a world architectural sense.

These buildings have been selected and photographed by the author Harry Sowden in an attempt to present evidence to suggest that the next epoch may be different from the previous two. There may be little real achievement in the work in this book but there is considerable promise indeed. Mies van der Rohe once said 'You only need ten (buildings) to change the cultural climate if they are good'. That this is possible is evidenced by small countries such as Finland. We can only impatiently wait and see.

Donald Gazzard

1.
The Early Australian Architects & Their Work by Morton Herman (Angus & Robertson)
2.
Walter Burley Griffin by James Birrell (Queensland University Press)
3.
The Australian Ugliness by Robin Boyd (Melbourne University Press)
4.
Harry Seidler (Horwitz Publications)

Rarely does a contemporary building provide an environment which is psychologically satisfactory for its occupants, without resort to handcraft materials. In Australia the 'craft' materials are frequently the most economical solution and, provided their use is in no way retrospective, then it may well be valid. However, we consider that one of the greatest challenges facing architects is the creation of an aesthetic using a truly twentieth century technology, which at the same time provides such a psychologically satisfactory environment.

The client must be a party to the design process in a more complete way than by merely stating his needs and criticizing the solution. By his constant contribution, coupled with his functional and psychological requirements, should come a thoughtful solution to his problem. Final aesthetic decisions must rest with the architect but, from the client's involvement, should emerge a basic expression of the building.

Design will always to some degree be conceptual, but the building, whilst of vital importance as pure architecture, is essentially shelter for a particular activity. As such it should not by its expression or character dominate that activity to its detriment. (An exhibition as architecture should not overpower the exhibits). To this extent our architectural approach could be deemed consequential.

It is hard to say with conviction that the buildings of our heritage have any direct influence on our work. We do appreciate the honest validity of early work here; its genuine ring of forthright building, coupled with a rugged elegance. It is asked, 'have we found an Australian vernacular expression?' This in effect is asking, 'can architecture today be regional rather than international?' The availability of materials, the climate, and even varying opinions related to similar problems, create different architectural solutions for similar building needs—thus influencing pure internationalism. In that we are Australians, working with Australians and striving for a genuine architecture, we could hope that, whilst in total aim our work is international, it is nevertheless Australian.

Clubbe Hall, Mittagong, NSW

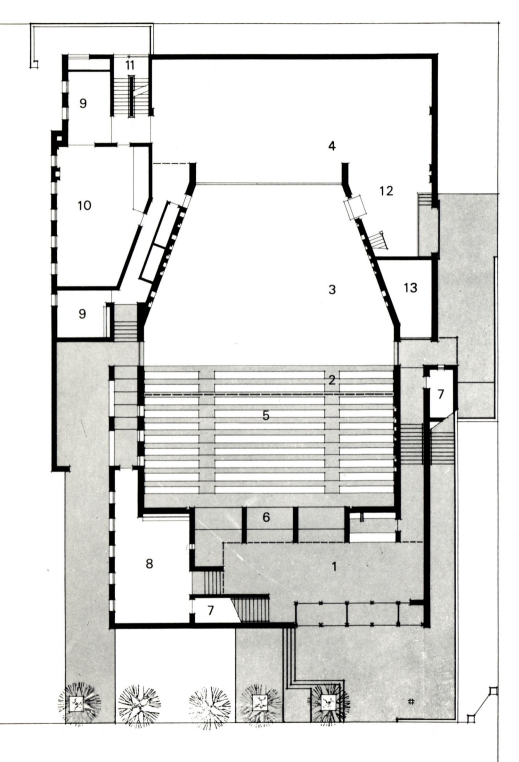

Clubbe Hall
Mittagong, NSW

Approximately eighty miles south-west
of Sydney, Clubbe Hall was built to
provide a theatre, hall and music rooms,
not only for Frensham Girls School
itself, but also to serve the district.

The hall was primarily planned for
assembly and theatre, but was also
required to satisfy the conflicting
acoustic needs of chamber music and
recitals.

The building is a simple but powerful
composition of brick planes and single
pitch tile roofs; much of its form being
dictated by the acoustic requirements
of the hall itself.

The local brick is used internally and
externally in walls and paving to reduce
maintenance and, at the same time, to
limit the vocabulary of materials.

1 foyer
2 auditorium—stepped section
3 auditorium—flat section
4 stage
5 gallery over
6 balcony over
7 store
8 general purpose
9 music rooms
10 orchestral practise room
11 up to dressing rooms
12 organ
13 chair store

10   0   30 FEET

Clubbe Hall, Mittagong, NSW

Sydney Ancher pioneered modern architecture in Sydney in the immediate post-war years. Joined by Bryce Mortlock and Stuart Murray, the firm gradually developed from the limited opportunities of domestic architecture. The practice expanded rapidly in 1964 and Ken Woolley joined the partnership. A major influence on the younger partners in their years of training was the work and attitude of Ancher himself, which not only embodied the principles of design being studied but also seemed to have a local character at a time when the design climate was all international style.

If it is accepted that local character derives from distinctive climate, distinctive materials both available and economical, and distinctive attitudes of the society, then any rational approach to architecture at this time should produce something identifiably Australian. Certain building types with lessons valid for today were very highly developed in Australia; notably nineteenth century industrial and public buildings, country functional tradition and the detached cottage. It follows that in similar buildings today this tradition should be evident.

-Some might argue that recent developments in communications, travel, international liaisons and building techniques will tend to break down any national architectural character which has emerged. It is quite possible however that more precise scientific methods of analyzing people's needs and responding to climatic and site problems will in fact create a different kind of distinctive regional character in architecture. Thus we may have regional rather than national identity in architecture. To implement this sort of approach the practice is organized so that with three active designing partners, individual but with common attitudes and consistent style, it enables selection of a designer fully involved in his work but serviced by the stability and depth made possible by a fairly large office.

For the future we believe it essential that Australians become more aware of the disadvantages of piecemeal small scale development. Two current projects, the Engineering Precinct at Sydney University and the twenty-seven acre Macquarie medium density housing group, have brought out the advantages for community, client and architecture of the design of the whole environment.

The Union, University of Newcastle, NSW

The Union
University of Newcastle, NSW

The Union is to form one side of the main central space at the new University of Newcastle. A later stage, three storeys high, will perform this task, hence the small scale of the present entrance, which is to face an inner court. The planning revolves around direct access from kitchen to major spaces, so that separate functions, complete with private courtyards, can take place at one time. The other spaces, common rooms, shops, offices, were also required on the one level, producing a building with an unusual variety of room sizes, heights and functions.

Materials are local brown brick and timber with quarry tile and carpet floors. Service and wet spaces are tiled and smooth plastered, curving up into the rooflight system.

Despite a potential for nostalgia in the traditional materials used, there is logic in the use of rational, traditional construction, so the exploiting of craft techniques for their aesthetic effect has been shunned and the abstract quality of openings, roof forms and details have been emphasized.

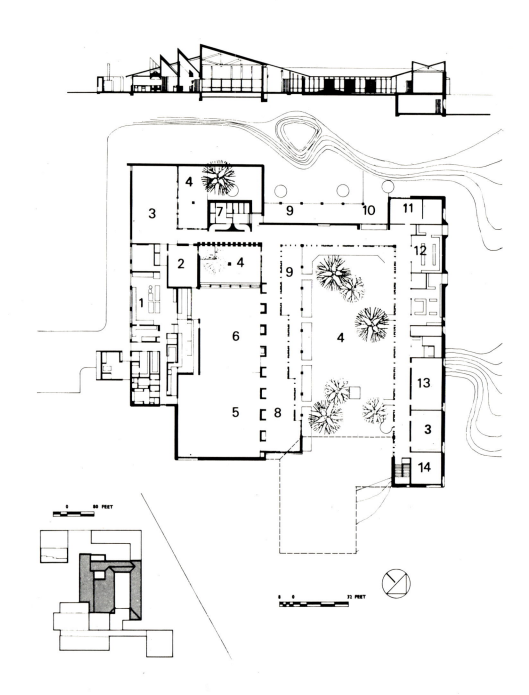

1 kitchens
2 DL McLarty room
3 common rooms
4 courtyards
5 dining room
6 coffee room
7 toilets
8 gallery
9 verandahs
10 entry
11 union office
12 shops and bank
13 reading room
14 meeting room

The Union, University of Newcastle, NSW

Great Hall
University of Newcastle, NSW

The winning entry in a limited competition, a memorable form which provides a visual impact at the central focal point of the University Plaza.

The inevitability of its three dimensional quality is the result of a design development from the interactions of numerous factors: site relationships and external circulation; the internal organization of different functions on interelated levels; the problem of site alignment (solved by a bent axis for internal circulation); the criteria of acoustic volumetrics; seating for 1500; gallery levels; escape stairs.

All these factors were fused together by a consistent design using external materials chosen for their affinity with existing buildings.

Project Housing

To consider the architect's role in this type of housing it is necessary to understand the change in production which has taken place. A few years ago there was a situation in which a small number of architect-designed, one-off houses influenced at rather long range the great mass of housing conforming with the current standards of fashion and popular taste. The house was built in a way which was increasingly left behind by other industries in development of management, production and marketing techniques. When architects were engaged they were responsible for designing, documenting and arranging for the construction for each house owner.

The advent of merchant building has meant a change in which the house has become more of a product in the sense of other manufactured items like washing machines or motor cars. The architect's services are thus oriented toward the producer. By this means good design reaches a greatly increased number of people and is now influencing the vernacular of building. Contractual and quality safeguards, for which the client looked to the architects, are now in the main provided by the demonstration houses, like the display models of any other product.

Pettit & Sevitt Project House
Wollstonecraft, NSW

'Gambrel' is, so far, the smallest in the range and, like the 'Lowline', is designed for unlimited extension and reversibility of parts of the plan. A very narrow plan and continuous window line give a larger impression to a 10 square (1,000 square feet) house. Roof is concrete tile on pre-fab trusses, walls brick veneer with plasterboard and timber interiors.

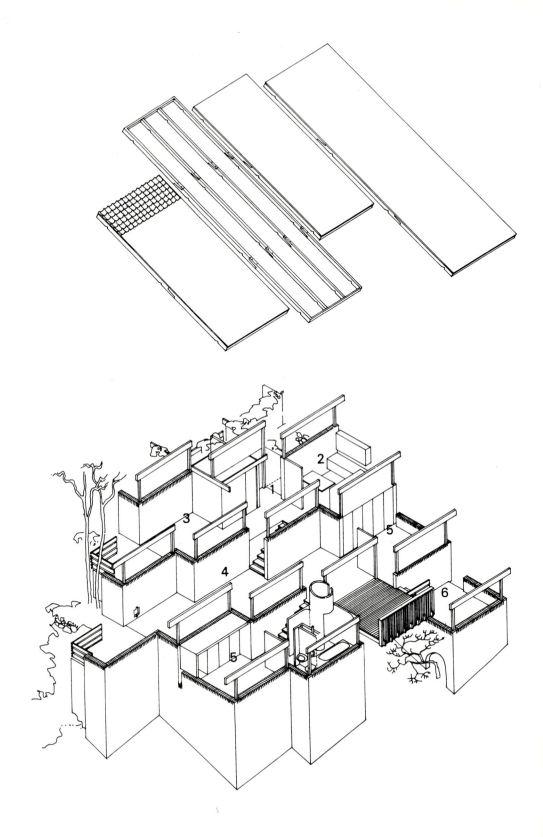

1 entry
2 kitchen
3 dining
4 lounge
5 bedrooms
6 study

House for Ken Woolley
Mosman, NSW

On a steep hillside, covered with large trees, rocks and ferns, and with an outlook over Middle Harbour, the design derives from an idea of garden terraces, part of which are covered by a massive timber roof sloping parallel to the land. A geometric discipline was imposed, the basis being a 12' 0'' square room, several of which are thrown together for the main central space. Each unit steps aside 4' 0'' following the land contours and the same one to three proportion is used for vertical separation. As each unit steps aside its roof is pulled away from the next one, creating narrow rooflights admitting leaf-filtered sunlight. Walls are clinker bricks, post and beam frame, infills timber, floors concrete covered with cork or matting.

Engineering Precinct
Sydney University, NSW

A site of between twelve and thirteen acres in the Special Uses Area of Darlington, lying roughly between City Road and Redfern Station, has been set aside by the University for the re-housing of the various departments of the Faculty of Engineering.

The first building, a Materials and Structures Testing Laboratory for the Department of Civil Engineering, was planned in 1959; the whole of Civil Engineering was completed by 1963. Then followed Chemical Engineering, Electrical Engineering and the first stage (two lecture theatres) of a Faculty Building. Planning has now begun for a complex to contain Mechanical and Aeronautical Engineering.

The final stage of the Faculty Building, already planned, will probably be built in 1970. A General Workshop is still to come and most of the buildings are designed for further extension.

Because of the long time span of the construction programme, the precinct character in the spaces between buildings has had little chance to develop as yet, but it is present in the overall plan and will appear as the building gaps are filled in.

Engineering Precinct,
Sydney University, NSW

This office normally consists of about twenty-five persons, and is constituted with a large proportion of young qualified architects and engineers as partners, associates and assistants, most of whom have worked or studied abroad at some stage during their association with the firm. As we are well aware of the architectural stimulus to be gained from overseas experience and outside architectural activities, it has been usual to find, in recent years, that at least one senior member of the firm has been overseas in this capacity at any one point of time.

While the external forms of our buildings vary greatly, we believe that an affinity exists in our design approach by the establishment of common rules governing planning, material selection and performance, with the endeavour to produce the pattern whereby simple and direct architectural statements can be made. The expression of our buildings is generally influenced by careful consideration of the climatic conditions of the region, together with the adoption of a concise structural system. The final design solutions are usually characterized by deeply recessed facades, a balanced relationship between solid and void with a consistency in the structural concept, and selection of materials being kept to a minimum wherever possible.

In the future we would like to see the office expanded by the introduction of more senior members who would be able to take an active part in the specialist roles that will be necessary to carry out the more complex building programme we can see eventuating in the next decade. We believe that an office kept to small numbers is still able to offer a comprehensive architectural service by employing and engaging specialist consultants, both internally and externally, who are well equipped to undertake the individual problems associated with many different building types, and resolving these in their own particular way.

Methodist Church, Bicton, WA

High School
South Fremantle, WA

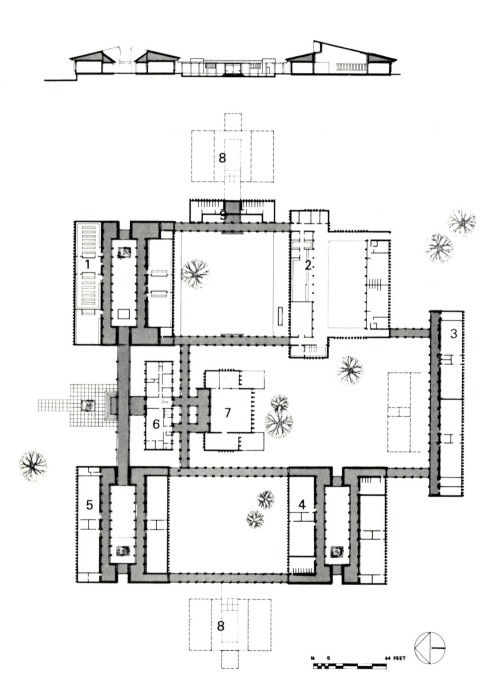

The High School, consisting basically of two materials, light cream bricks to all walls externally and internally, and orange tiled roofs, is planned to extend to its ultimate development in four separate stages. Each of the main departments—Science, Home Science, Arts and Crafts, and Classroom Houses—are included in completely separate buildings, whose rooms enclose colonnaded courtyards.

These courtyards provide congregation spaces protected from the winter winds and summer sun and are inter-connected by a series of covered ways enclosing larger courts or open spaces, of varying size, which provide visual variety.

1 science laboratory wing
2 general purpose area
3 manual training wing
4 art and craft wing
5 home science and classroom wing
6 administration block
7 library
8 future classrooms
9 toilets

16 0   64 FEET

High School, South Fremantle, WA

William Padbury Centre
Perth, WA

Three storey professional offices 63' 0''
square, with perimeter offices arranged
around a centrally located service core.
Full height precast concrete columns
support the projecting concrete flat
plate floors, and precast sunhoods
afford reasonable sun and glare protection on all facades within the frame-
work of a consistent structural expression.

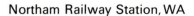
Northam Railway Station, WA

A new station and District Administrative Offices in the wheat-belt country town of Northam, for the Western Australian Government Railways Commission. This station forms part of the standard gauge railway project at present under construction from Kalgoorlie to Perth. The building is carried on a concrete frame for the basement, ground and first floor slabs, which support a 6' 0'' cantilevered administrative floor incorporating precast concrete sills, fascias, columns, and sunhoods protecting a deeply recessed façade.

**Caradoc Ashton, Fisher, Woodhead & Beaumont Smith
Adelaide, South Australia**

The average age of the principals of the firm is forty years, all are South Australian born and all have received their architectural education at the local Schools of Architecture. The original partners who founded the firm in 1927 were trained in the first architectural school in South Australia, at what was then known as the South Australian School of Mines and Industries.

Throughout the history of the firm all types of commissions have been accepted, but past and present job lists illustrate a preponderance of industrial, commercial and institutional-type buildings.

From its inception this firm has endeavoured to approach design, constructional, and administrative problems from a local point of view, a view naturally guided and prompted by current trends, modern thought and modern materials, but not bound by outside fashions and influences. Contributions to progressive Australian architecture are made with both sensitive and competent constructional detailing directly related to the economic and geographical brief.

Why should Australian architects be influenced in design by the stimulus induced by the threat of world population explosion? Why conceive of a multi-celled vertical complexity of ants' nests when these architects be-

lieve the real problem is to produce buildings to satisfy the combined factors of under-population and over-centralization, while allowing for an orderly accelerating growth rate? Should not architects always analyze their designs to determine whether regional factors have been properly considered? Why design a multi-acred factory with an unlit flat roof when South Australian skies offer an excellent daylight factor? Why force the use of harsh sunscreens in areas where, in many cases, there is still room for trees? Why select the glamorous or popular foreign material when a similar result can be obtained from the cheaper local material characteristic of the area? Why contort the plan and elevational shapes to achieve notoriety?

This group of Adelaide architects believes that it can contribute more and more to an Australian architecture freer of local and international clichés, and looks forward to a growing case history of completed works illustrating straight-forward functional planning, uncluttered design concepts, good detailing, and sound construction using economical materials with Australian methods.

Chrysler Australia Ltd, Adelaide, SA

Chrysler Australia Limited
Adelaide, SA

The requirements of the plant were: Stamping Plant and Assembly Shop of 1,000,000 sq.ft for production of 200 vehicles a day; Associated Tool Room, Plating Shop, Boiler House and ancillaries; Cafeteria with capacity of 1,100 persons a shift; Distribution Building for local sales; Engineering and Experimental Centre of 60,000 sq.ft; Administration Building of 60,000 sq.ft.

Selection of the site was made with particular reference to space for immediate programme plus extensive requirement for future expansion, adjacency to rail and road transport services, adjacency to high density housing areas, adequate public utility services, landscaping potential, and secreted spaces available for employee and new vehicle parking.

First work on the site commenced Easter 1963. First sections of the plant were in operation Easter 1964 and the total plant was completed by January 1966. All buildings are of large span steel frame construction, using off-site prefabrication techniques to the maximum. Walling components are generally precast concrete, asbestos cement sheet, asbestos aggregate sheet and brick, with aluminium frame window components.

Chrysler Australia Ltd, Adelaide, SA

Chrysler Australia Ltd, Adelaide, SA

Architecture means so many things to so many men that we have come to distrust lengthy philosophies about Architecture, Society and the Cosmos. Although stimulating, CIAM Manifestos and Delos Declarations have a limited usefulness. The environments of our cities are deteriorating so rapidly and urban problems are so complex, that we cannot continue to think of architecture in terms of isolated monuments.

We hold an unwavering belief in the importance of the trust we hold from Society with our architectural and environmental work. In our changing situation, we believe, this trust can only be discharged by extending and integrating our traditionally limited architectural field with other separate but related disciplines.

The activities of our group range from basic urban research and economic studies, through physical planning and the design of buildings, to interior and landscape design. Some of us have backgrounds in fields like geography and engineering rather than architecture; we find the labels unimportant but the interaction fruitful. We think this range of operations is necessary if we are eventually going to create environments rather than separate buildings.

We like to think we are realists as well as idealists. If planning a new town or building a redevelopment calls for creative thinking in solving legal, administrative or financial problems, or involvement in the politics of citizen participation, then these have to be as much part of our brief as the design of the buildings if we are to succeed.

However, it's not what you say but the way that you say it, as the song says, and we prefer to try to cope with our times of growth and change and be judged by our work. That built is limited in its range as the partnership only began in 1960 on the return of George Clarke and myself to Australia after six years working and studying in other continents. Through lack of opportunity, our built work does not yet accurately reflect our belief in the central impact of technology on our buildings.

Donald Gazzard

Baby Health Centre, Pennant Hills, NSW

Mona Vale Community Centre
Mona Vale, NSW

These community buildings are situated between two scattered, sprawling suburban shopping streets. The small Baby Health Centre had to be built several years earlier than the Community Hall, and a small Children's Library has still to be built to complete the group.

The architectural aim was to create a 'village centre' that would join the separated shopping streets by spaces which would be walked through and provide an *agora* pivot for community life. The Baby Health Centre has its own forecourt, where small children can play safely, while waiting for their mothers.

Low cost, low maintenance materials with natural finishes were used throughout the building and the structure is frankly exposed. Natural lighting and cross ventilation in the hall are assisted by a continuous skylight, running the full length of the hall.

Wentworth Memorial Church
Vaucluse, NSW

This church, built on a strict budget to seat 350, is sited on the top of a magnificent sandstone acropolis that rises out of an old harbourside suburb in Sydney.

The ideas of the New Liturgical Movement were strongly held. The congregation has been brought close to the sanctuary in a way determined to increase the feeling of direct participation and lessen the feeling of remoteness felt in older churches.

The natural lighting of new churches in countries with strong sunlight is usually badly handled. Here the light suffuses the church indirectly from a skylight hidden high over the sanctuary. The superb site has been exploited with a Martiennsen eye to Greek subtlety, with a strong feeling that such buildings should be approached, walked through and traversed with varying rapport between the different spatial changes. There is no static Renaissance viewpoint here.

1 forecourt
2 porch
3 font
4 350 seats
5 pulpit
6 choir and organ
7 vestry

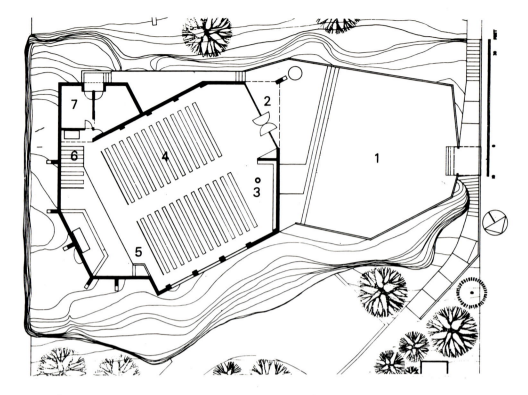

Wentworth Memorial Church, Vaucluse, NSW

Shopping Centre
Hornsby, NSW

An extension of a suburban shopping area consisting of a large supermarket and seventeen smaller shops. The supermarket is an air conditioned brick box standing on an off-form concrete plinth.

Access to all the shops is from an enclosed central mall that joins the main street frontage to a rear parking area. The central part is raised to allow the pivotal centre court to have a larger volume daylit by clearstorey windows.

Materials internally are natural cedar boarded ceilings, red quarry tile paving and glazed shop-fronts with black anodized aluminium frames and white ceramic tile and face brick panels.

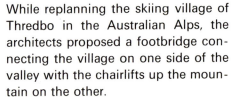

Timber Footbridge
Thredbo, NSW

While replanning the skiing village of Thredbo in the Australian Alps, the architects proposed a footbridge connecting the village on one side of the valley with the chairlifts up the mountain on the other.

The bridge is 8' 0'' wide and 180' 0'' long and is made of Alpine Ash, an Australian hardwood. The timber supports were raked to obtain the dual benefit of reducing the span of the bridge beams and minimizing the number of ground supports, the location of which were limited by the river and road which the bridge had to cross.

By raking the supports, it was also possible to obtain the benefits of a rigid frame in resisting horizontal loads on the bridge, without requiring rigid connections between columns and beams, which are difficult to obtain in timber structures.

Housing

Australian cities have the lowest densities in the world—the normal suburban house has an average site area of over quarter of an acre—and it is only recently that the resultant geographic sprawl has caused a higher proportion of Australians to look favourably on living in other forms of more compact housing.

The main factor that differentiates this type of housing from its European counterparts, and that complicates life for the designer, is the high rate of car ownership which is second only to North America. This high use of cars has been enjoyed in a low density situation for some time and it is now regarded by most Australians as a fifth freedom that they be allowed to drive their cars everywhere—even right up to their living room door. Site planning tends therefore to be automobile dominated and visually rather exploded.

The first stage in the redevelopment of the twenty-nine acre inner area, known as the St James Glebe, at Edgecliff, three miles from the centre of Sydney, is just about to commence. The photograph shown gives little idea of the topographic challenge and possibilities of the site which falls 150 feet across its length and breadth. The residential sections pivot around a megastructure of underground railway station, bus terminal, department store, shops and offices, with integrated levels of parking.

Town Houses, Sydney, NSW

Architecture cannot be confined within frontiers whether they be geographical, economic, or social, and change is the constant; interaction, innovation, revolution is the norm.

The new World View of thoughtful people demands a revaluation of the existing Australian scene. To most of us, Australia is still an open society blessed with opportunities for individuals to develop, and where anyone can indulge his fancy and live under the sun. No-one, however, pretends that this is going to last indefinitely, and the changes that will reform architects and architecture are already evident in the ideas of some individuals. But, in the main, the whole situation is lacking when compared with other developed countries. For example, one-off housing reeks of the wrong sort of individualism, and cluster, patio or high density housing in Australian cities is rare.

City redevelopment, generally, is baroque in character and quite out of touch with tomorrow's demands. Technology is misunderstood and rarely applied comprehensively. System building is in its infancy and waits nervously on the sidelines for permission to participate.

Paradoxically, like all Australian architects, I know this state of affairs cannot continue and yet I find it hard to regret these last ten years designing individual houses.

In Queensland, with climate as the central discipline, to build in the sun is stimulating. The magic of sun and shadow soon captures your senses and directs you towards worthwhile solutions. But to dispense comfort and happiness through useful form in one-off housing is not enough, and we all anticipate a wider area of involvement for architects in the future.

House at Indooroopilly, Qld

House at Toowong for
R. Graham

Design for climate in the hot humid sub-tropical areas of Queensland demands northern orientation for all major rooms, and cross ventilation from north east prevailing breezes.

A basic sensibility in the creation of space suited to climatic conditions determines roof forms, for example, that incorporate air extracts set along the roof ridge.

Deep shade, large overhangs, and louvred and screened openings result in a regional expression. As technological innovation is marginal, traditional building methods are utilized.

This family required a budget house with minimum of three bedrooms, and planned for future family room. Due to incidence of mosquitoes and other insects, fly screening to outdoor living areas was requested.

Materials are white-painted common bagged brickwork, sawn Queensland Box hardwood weatherboards, creosote stained, white concrete roofing tiles, Queensland Pink Box timber flooring, sliding frameless $\frac{1}{4}''$ drawn glass windows, plasterboard and oiled weatherboard wall and ceiling linings.

House at Toowong, Qld

House at Kenmore for
Mrs E. M. Leitch

The site is five acres of cleared bush-land, falling steeply to the Brisbane River to the south. The client and her husband, retired, wished to build a home which would provide amenities for today's living but with the ability to house existing family furniture. Mr Leitch, who had spent a great part of his life in Western Queensland in the pastoral industry, favoured a design with large internal volume and deep verandahs.

The long, low expression of this house embodies design characteristics of the region: 8' 0" wide verandahs, gal-vanized steel hoods over the windows, batten screens to verandah ends, roof cripples to accommodate high internal ceilings and low verandahs all natur-ally evolved out of the client's requests. The older furniture, and the interesting collection of a Queensland family's lifetime, have been enclosed in a form that succeeds in relating to the personal and private lives of the occupants.

Materials are white-painted common bagged brickwork, Brown Alder cham-ferboards, oil finish, white concrete roofing tiles, reinforced concrete sub-floor, with carpet and cork tile finish, Spotted Gum sawn roof rafters, ex-posed throughout the house forming trusses, brick paving to the verandah.

House at Indooroopilly for
P. Rabaa

An average site with north western slope and narrow street frontage. The client's requirements were similar to those of the Grahams, but with a more predominant brick construction and long northern verandah.

The design is a strong regional form with crippled roof over the verandah. Roof ventilators give similar ventilation to that of the Grahams. The large verandah provides summer living area that is extensively used by the owners and, being 8′ 0″ wide, provides deep shade to all major rooms. The exposed roof rafters in the interior and sawn weatherboard wall linings impart a strong character.

Materials are white-painted common bagged brickwork, sawn Queensland Ironbark weatherboards, creosote stained, white concrete roofing tiles, Queensland Tallowwood timber flooring to verandah, sliding frameless $\frac{1}{4}$″ drawn glass windows, plasterboard and oiled weatherboard walls, exposed roof trusses and sawn Red River Gum rafters.

House at Toowong for
P. G. Wilson

On a steep northern slope, on a two and a half acre property, the family required a four-bedroomed house with family room, double bathroom, atrium screened entertaining area, to be totally flyscreened, and with private sun-bathing courtyard adjacent to bathrooms. The plan is similar to the Graham house, but more extensive (climate is the constant in design factors). Through ventilation to rooms on the south side is provided by 8' 0" long metal louvre at the roof, hence the roof form. The tiled atrium proved to be a useful breezeway and entertaining area on hot, humid nights. Landscaping was extensive and the architectural qualities are now made more effective by subtle screening and lush vegetation as counterpoint to the linear discipline of the form.

Materials are concrete masonry block, Queensland Hardwood chamferboards, rolled galvanized steel deck roofing, plasterboard and oiled chamferboard walls, 'Woodtex' ceiling, sliding frameless ¼" drawn glass windows.

Architecture expresses our culture. Whether we like it or not, is is unavoidably portrayed. Developing parallel with our scientific/technocratic age, overawed by the machine, mirroring its philosophy it has, in the post war decades, blatantly proclaimed an indifference to human organic needs and purposes. This package architecture, sterile to the life it should sustain and elevate, touched off reactions.

Lacking spiritual nourishment in our contemporary environment, other cultures were investigated in history and literature—to assimilate the desired feelings of historical continuity; to give our buildings a presence in time—to verify a philosophy justifying organic functions and the significance of life; to express the dignity of man. Architecture's highest order should be the art of transforming man's entire habitat. Imagination, the basis of all creation, is abundant, but it withers for want of exercise, discouraged by the so-called practical man. Confronted by a money economy as opposed to a life economy, planning for the benefit of the community is frustrated, fragmented and dissonant.

The return to organic evolution which is cumulative and purposeful recreates a visible architectural force seeking a new synthesis—new attempts to invoke the universal grammar of architecture, the infinite variety of geometry, the understanding of pure design integrated to human needs, the rejection of preconceptions. It subjugates science/technology to its rightful station; uses it to serve, not dominate its expression. Values are reversed. Integrity emerges with new meaning.

Buildings are integral with environment, with function, with purpose and the nature of materials. Quality precedes quantity. The organic order is based on variety, complexity and balance. Like the ancient alchemists, architects must transmute these thoughts to architecture. Buildings should speak to the soul of man and also let him in.

C. Madigan

Library, Dee Why, NSW

Library
Dee Why, NSW

Client's requirements: A central lending library to house 45,000 books, with pre-fixed cost limits. The library was designed as an element of a civic centre that may be built on the plateau behind the new building. The architectural forms, a direct interpretation of programme and function, seek to establish a civic place—an urban core for the rapidly expanding Warringah Shire.

The open site on a rising slope above a public parking area has a setting of giant weathered sandstone rocks. The colours of the building blend with the scene. Brick forms cradle the suspended exposed aggregate concrete panels which wrap around the building, enclosing the main space. This concrete band floats above a continuous ribbon window. On the north and south sides of the building the sloping roofed annexes trap sunlight and reflect it into the book stack areas.

The southern entrance has step and ramp approach from the car park forecourt—one proceeds under a low gallery into the main space. The top entrance, with no steps, is from the access way to the future civic centre hill site.

In sympathy with the sloping site, the planning is organized on three levels. Different ceiling heights, creating interesting spacial contrasts, flow into each other; the main reading well with high ceilings is surrounded by galleries, and all levels are interconnected by ramps and steps. A control point is located in the centre of this building and brings all using the library to the charging desk. This is on the mid-level and has visual control over the whole library. Apart from the entrance floors which are brick paved, all areas are covered in a stippled blue-black carpet. Light is from roof skylights and night lighting duplicates the natural source. The interior is predominantly white relieved by off-white gloss on the exposed structural steel elements and a dark cordovan brown on the sloping ceiling of the northern annex. The Tasmanian Oak timber lining boards and doors are grey wax stained. Furniture, designed by the architects, has bright chrome accents with beige and black covers.

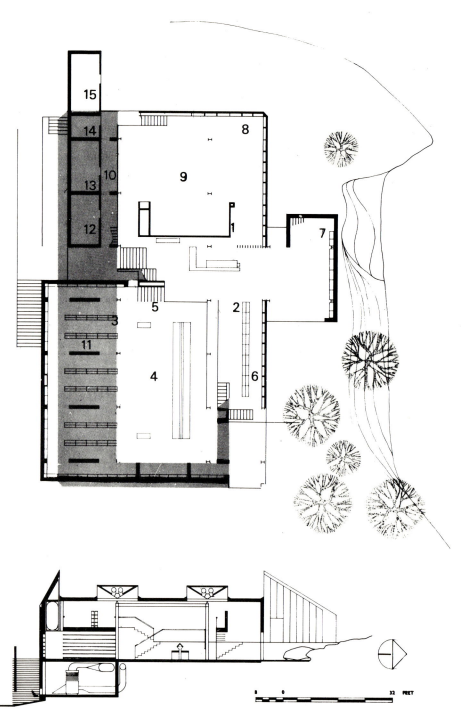

1 control centre
2 reference library
3 adult library
4 reading room
5 catalogue
6 lounge
7 periodicals
8 workroom
9 compactus
10 toilets
11 children's library (gallery)
12 easy books (gallery)
13 chief librarian (gallery)
14 deputy librarian (gallery)
15 staff room

Library, Dee Why, NSW

The Victorian scene is changing. As architects, we are less dominated by the expedient needs of a pioneering economy to provide basic shelter. No longer are we isolated from the dialogue of contemporary societies in other parts of the world. This new sophistication has led to an awareness of values other than the merely utilitarian and economic. This attitude is reflected in greater refinement within the architectural disciplines.

We aim simply to provide good conscientious architecture neither fashionable nor doctrinaire. It results, we hope, from an aim to create structure well and unaffectedly from the ground up, using simple, unadorned natural materials with simple connections, thus imposing an artistic order after examining each relational problem of space, structure, services, materials, climate and environment from scratch.

In this way, a particular pattern of structural theme most suited to the problem is discovered. Elements interfering with this theme are rejected. This 'artistic order' is followed through into the relationships of the spaces between buildings, and the opportunity to exercise this order has been found in a number of our university projects. This order is of course severely subjective and we hope successful in the terms of the special accord established between a client and ourselves.

The observer may not always share the terms of these subjective decisions.

The office in Melbourne is of medium size, with a branch office in Canberra, and consists of several teams under partners' control. In addition to our Australian architects, we have colleagues from the United Kingdom, Europe and Asia who contribute by widening the design perspective.

Alexander Theatre,
Monash University, Vic

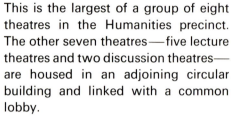

Alexander Theatre
Monash University
Melbourne, Vic

This is the largest of a group of eight theatres in the Humanities precinct. The other seven theatres—five lecture theatres and two discussion theatres—are housed in an adjoining circular building and linked with a common lobby.

Although primarily designed for public lectures, the theatre and extensive fly tower cater for three basic types of drama: standard theatre requiring proscenium stage, theatre in the round and Elizabethan type theatre with peninsular stage.

A large forestage lift permits rapid change of use and also makes provision for an orchestra pit. Permanent seating is 508 but an additional 200 seats may be added in accordance with required usage.

Walls internally are precast prestressed concrete with superimposed boxes housing Helmsholtz resonators, amplifiers and stage lighting. Walls externally are brick. Fly tower is clad with precast exposed quartz aggregate concrete slabs.

Architect's Office
Melbourne, Vic

Planned by Eggleston, Macdonald and Secomb for their own use. The majority of the work space is on level two and is air conditioned and dust free. The drawing office is in one large area, subdivided into bays with movable benches and screens, and offices for associates, specification writers and technical library to one side.

Level one accommodates car park, entrance foyer, conference room and toilets.

The structure is buff coloured sand blasted concrete. Walls are concrete block. Windows are grey heat absorbing glass set in western red cedar frames. The metal deck roof is supported on timber joists and boxed steel portal frames. Compressed straw board panels form the ceiling.

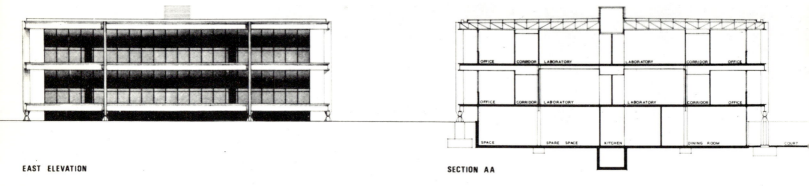

EAST ELEVATION

SECTION AA

| OFFICE | CORRIDOR | LABORATORY | | LABORATORY | CORRIDOR | OFFICE |
| OFFICE | CORRIDOR | LABORATORY | | LABORATORY | CORRIDOR | OFFICE |

SPACE   SPARE SPACE   KITCHEN   DINING ROOM   COURT

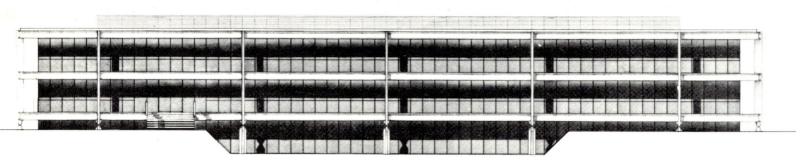

NORTH ELEVATION

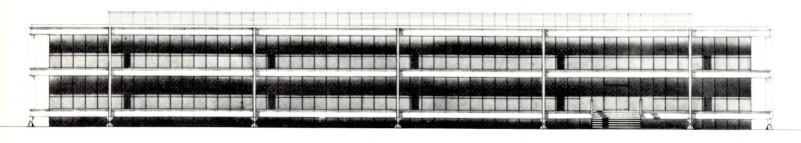

SOUTH ELEVATION

LABORATORY BLOCK

BHP Melbourne
Research Laboratories

The first stage of a research centre for
the activities of Australia's largest company, The Broken Hill Proprietary
Company Limited, consists of a laboratory building and technological buildings concerned with steel production.

Steel is strongly expressed in the exposed frame of Aus-Ten 50 steel which
develops a corrosion resistant soft
brown texture requiring no painting.

The recessed face of the building will
be a grey bronze heat absorbing glass
set in Aus-Ten steel mullions.

The laboratory building was planned
on a ring corridor principle with a compact and easily serviced internal core
surrounded by research offices.

It is fully air conditioned and designed
to meet the changing needs of the
Company and new developments in
research equipment.

Robin Gibson   Brisbane, Queensland

In a continent where it is difficult to hide in antiquity and where it is even more difficult to draw from the past architectural development, it is necessary to create and evolve a strength of purpose in all forms of architectural design. The need for creating a fresh and original approach is born from the same mould as the Australian bushman and his trust in the final proof of the basic solution to the problem.

From this birth the creation of all work begins with the rationalization and eventual abstraction of all problems, then the re-creation and personal emotional involvement with the architect. Together with the continuity of past experiences, these simple truths amalgamate collectively to create a virile and truthful architecture for a young and growing country.

In a country which offers a landscape ranging from tropic lushness of vibrant colours to the dry monotony of the monochromatic plains, you are constantly aware of the presence of magnificent light and its ever changing values. The control of this light and the plays of shadows and the emotional results all join to produce a young architecture, involving people in a young country.

In retrospect this work is not seen as an emerging distinctive school of Australian architecture, but as a design process which is ever changing and ever expanding in light of improved techniques and technologies; the paramount energy for the work being the importance of the providing of the correct environmental control for the benefit of the people and for the various design problems posed.

The Gourmet, Brisbane, Qld

The Gourmet
Brisbane, Qld

Described in the dictionaries as 'a nice feeder; an epicure' the word conjures up a host of pleasantries; the varied and glorious colours of food, the smell of fresh cooked food, the involvement of people and their habits.

Against this background, this take away food operation was created in waxed white pine boarded ceilings, polished copper counters and hygienic scrubbable floors and walls, an open visual kitchen at the rear of the store.

Except for the graphics which consist of an illuminated awning fascia and incised lettering burnt into the pine doors, the remainder of the imagery is left to the food and the gourmets.

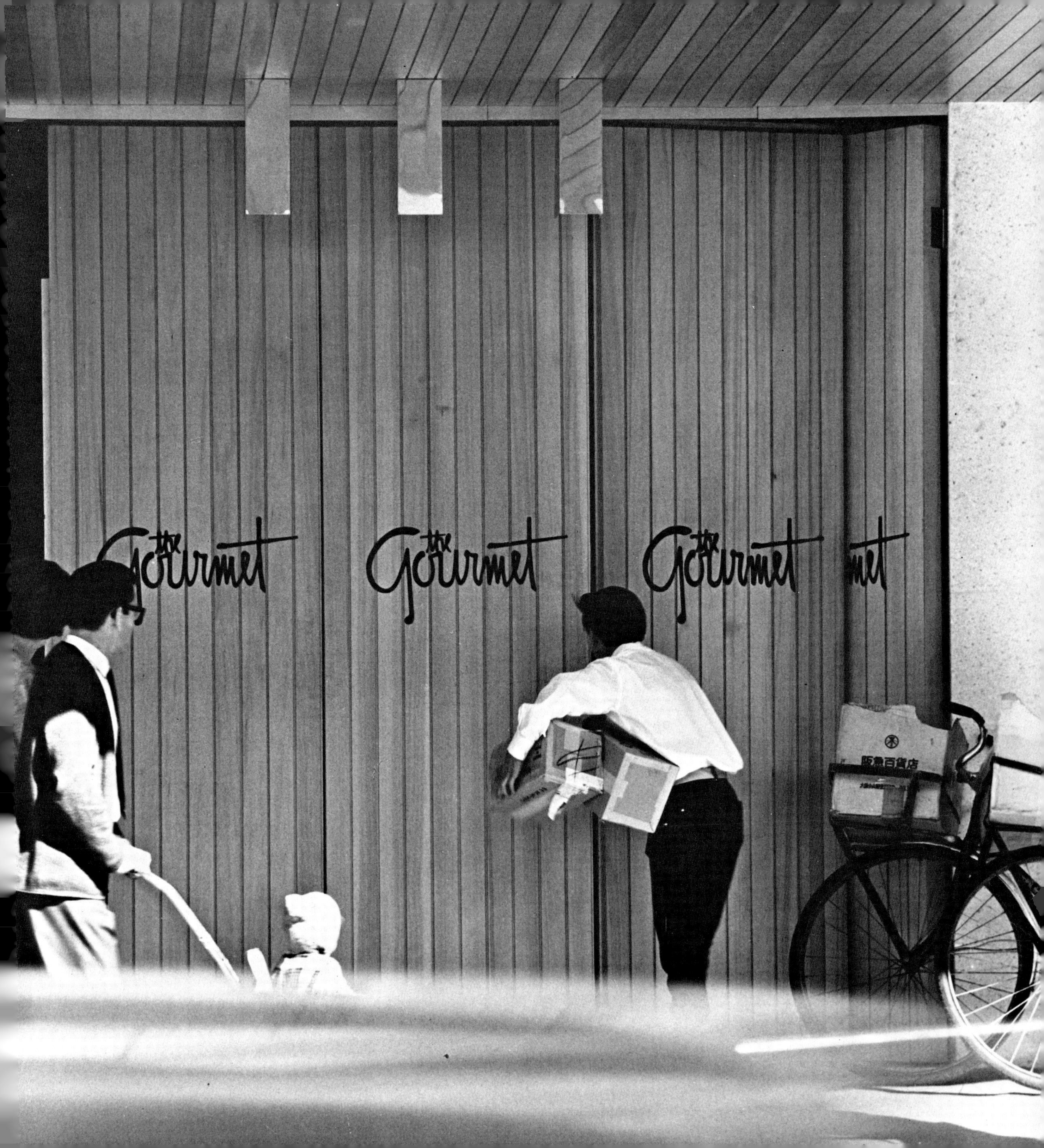
the Gourmet
the Gourmet
the Gourmet
阪急百貨店

The Gourmet, Brisbane, Qld

Bulk Storage Facilities
Pinkenba, Qld

Set in an industrial area at the mouth
of the Brisbane River, these additions
to the bulk handling facilities for the
State Wheat Board express the various
processes involved in the storage and
handling of the wheat.

This expression is delineated by the
grouping of the separate functional
elements in a sculptural solution.

Bulk Storage, Pinkenba, Qld

The four 60 feet diameter slip form concrete silos, supported on piles, rise to a conical top supporting the square form of the Silo House. The 3' 0" deep waffle slab, which is supported at four points, cantilevers 30' 0" in two directions.

The tall shaft of the working house, designed in structural steel and clad in off-white steel sheeting, houses fumigation dust collection and the elevators, and is expressed as an isolated element. The precise form provides an articulate contrast to the softer cylindrical forms of the silos.

This vertical shaft has been turned at 45 degrees to the axis of the silos for simple right-angle connections with the gantries.

The continuous fenestration to the Silo House and working houses, punctuated only on the eastern side of the Silo House by necessity to provide for future expansion, allows the roofs and cladding materials to be read as elements visually divorced from the structure.

My private practice was established in 1962 in the supposedly normal Australian fashion, with plenty of enthusiasm, plenty of debts, no capital and a solitary client.

Since practising architecture my principle has been that, for every job, an attempt must be made to produce good architecture, and I believe that if this attempt is not made the creative capacity will decrease, resulting in unimaginative and mundane work. In Australia, where cross stimulation is scarce due to distance, it is necessary for the architect to have integrity in this regard for him to continually do creative work, and every potential dilution of his principles must be thwarted.

Obviously creative capacity exists in a number of unheralded Australian architects but, because their genes are presumed to be similar to those of architects of the previous generation they are generally processed to follow a similar pattern of architectural development. Disillusionment follows and he either sacrifices his earlier principles to concentrate on making money, or accepts the role of a poorly paid idealist, battling with small houses and alterations, to finally deliver himself to a budget-paying, large, amorphous, so-called architectural firm.

None of these paths are particularly healthy and certainly they will not provide the stimulus needed to produce good architecture over a long period. However, if the architect retains his integrity and drive, his achievements and his importance to the community will increase.

Architectural integrity does not imply that an egomaniac is at large, prepared to sink his teeth into every client who is not in accord with his every whim. Instead, it is an adherence to principles relative to the individual, and the intelligent application of these principles injected with a balanced dose of imagination, intuition, emotion and common sense to a client's problems should produce an excellent form of architecture.

The commonsense factor is critical because it is the basis of truthful transition from a problem to a solution. It is necessary to all functional architecture, and its constant usage, in initiating experimental developments with local materials in local environments, should eventually establish indigenous forms of architecture.

Merchant Builders House, Melbourne, Vic

Merchant Builders

In 1965 I was commissioned by Merchant Builders Pty Ltd to design a range of project houses commencing with three basic elements, each capable of six variations. These are now constructed on the owners' land at a cost between $10,000 and $16,000 after the owners have selected their house type from a display group.

The Builders have an enlightened and uncompromising approach — both being very rare traits in Australia. Their potential as a sympathetic development group is beyond question and they are as interested in experimentation (if well directed) and architectural advancement as their architect.

They believe that co-ordination between themselves and all related fields of activity is essential and, to this end, the architect is retained to carry out all drawings and to control all design sequences. A landscape designer has been commissioned to provide sympathetic environments for their buildings, and graphic artists in conjunction with a photographer carry out all advertising and display work. In all of these fields the Builders have attempted to obtain the best service possible.

Merchant Builders House, Melbourne, Vic

STUDIO

COURTYARD AND TERRACE HOUSES BY MERCHANT BUILDERS
CNR. THE BOULEVARD AND SPRINGVALE ROAD GLEN WAVERLY

PROJECT
HOUSES

Pine Mont Pre-School
Ringwood, Vic

The building had to be designed within some rather archaic and restrictive health regulations, the most crippling being a height minimum which seemed more suitable to giants than children. As an answer to this problem, the height of the internal spaces was visually reduced by averaging out the main playroom space from a high roof light to door height at the perimeter and also by extending the sloping roof beyond the wall lines. The apparent ignorance of the Health Authorities of the ways in which children play naturally again influenced the playground, where earth banks more than 3' 0'' high had to be provided with balustrades to protect the children.

The construction is a dual timber post and beam system with external metal wall panels and roofing and, where possible, natural finished hardboard internally.

Shoebridge House
Doncaster East, Vic

A pine forest was a strong influence on
the design of this house for a family
which included four young children.
Strong rough sawn timbers are used
for a post and beam structure and infill
cladding. These are all stained to match
the colour of the pine trees. The house
is large and low, with a simple pitched
iron roof and a similar shaped floor
soffit which houses a central heating
duct running the length of the house.
The floor is one level except for the
entry and carport which sit under the
house where the ground line falls away.

Internally, the space is continuous
except where sliding semi-transparent
screens are used to separate the children's sleeping area from the gallery
and the dining and living rooms. All
lighting other than that necessary for
local work is concealed either between
or behind beams to accentuate the
subdued atmosphere.

Australian architecture is going through a period of finding its own identity, the dictating factors being climatical and economical. In every job we do, no matter whether it is a house or a huge office building, the over-riding consideration is cost. It has to be economical, it has to be absolutely minimum cost, so we try to design directly, simply and economically.

In Perth we are considered to be one of the bigger firms but, by general standards, we are fairly small. We are designing buildings for a very high temperature range here in Western Australia—severe driving rains and cold in winter and, in the other extreme, long periods of intense heat in summer. The problems of expansion and contraction and waterproofing are very real, along with sea air corrosion in many cases. We must design for minimum maintenance because, in a young country like this, people do not have a lot of money to spend keeping their buildings in good condition. They would far rather have a building that requires nothing to be done to it, so materials have to be completely maintenance free as far as possible.

At the outset of a job, when it is at the design stage, we are thinking of the client's requirements, of the climate in all its extremes, of the maintenance and care of the building after it is built, and of the capabilities of the builder. The buildings that result always seem straight-forward. We are not attempting to beat the world with our design, just to give the client something he can happily use in the way he wants.

Beach Kiosk, Cottesloe, WA

Beach Kiosk
Cottesloe, WA

This small building provides facilities for patrons of the Eric Street beach, one of the most popular in the Perth metropolitan area. The kiosk stocks picnic foodstuffs and has easy access at road level, with a large paved area surrounded by seats. Changing rooms with normal toilet and washing facilities are underneath, at beach level. A large flight of concrete steps provides the main access to the beach.

The major design consideration was the need to withstand wear from coastal weather and public alike. Although small, the building was founded on piles driven down to the rock so that, in winter storm erosion, it would not be washed away like its timber predecessor. The general construction, including counter, is of concrete and concrete block.

Beach Kiosk, Cottesloe, WA

Walkway
Cottesloe, WA

The purpose of the walkway is to take the general public using Cottesloe beach as easily and directly as possible from change rooms, beach restaurants and shopping areas to the stone groyne. This groyne was erected several years ago to protect the beach and to try to prevent its continued erosion. This has been successful but the level of the groyne was, of course, higher than the normal beach level.

This work was again carried out in concrete for the purpose of standing up to normal weather and to excessive storms. It is all supported on driven concrete piles and the walkway itself and its railings are also concrete. A wider area was made about half way to the groyne so that a band or other entertainment could perform on it. Concrete steps lead down from this to the beach level.

It is a fairly simple and direct construction and was laid out on a general curve to follow the natural layout of the beach, and to attempt to enclose it a little. The area under the walkway is used as a sun shelter.

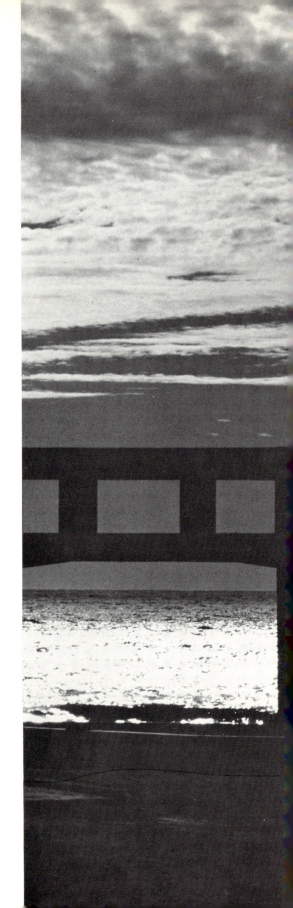

Walkway, Cottesloe, WA

School for Deaf Children
Mosman, WA

Eight additional classrooms were required, as an addition to an existing school consisting of a number of converted old brick buildings.

The site is right on the coast and very exposed, necessitating materials as resistant to weather deterioration as possible. Because of this, and to avoid undue damage by children, we used in-situ concrete. To complement the surrounding clean, white beaches, we chose white rather than the duller grey.

The form of the building was kept as simple and direct as possible so that it fitted in with the existing buildings on the site.

Classroom size was laid down at about 22' 0" x 18' 0" and had to have large areas of blackboard as the children see rather than hear. They also required mirrors for studying their lip movements.

A plain poured concrete roof, treated only with Caltite to keep it weatherproof, has been most successful.

School for Deaf Children, Mosman, WA

We see the participation of the architect to be vital to the future structure of society in an explosive second half of this century. There is a need to gear ourselves to the escalating advances of science and technology, the political machines and the take-over systems of living; to size up and cope with new frontiers which are changing so rapidly that they are often hard to fully comprehend.

It is our aim to let every building discover itself and be moulded for its particular purpose, whether it be for work or play, buying or selling, for living, for worship, for teaching. We gain pleasure from the continuous task of moulding, re-evaluating and consolidating our thinking with great enthusiasm for today and tomorrow.

To meet the sheer physical needs of the community, efficient planning should be taken for granted. We want our work to be something more. We believe it is vital we do not lose the human qualities so essential to personal appreciation, qualities in which people find continued interest and happiness. We are deeply concerned with environment, and design to build simply and economically, using materials intended to evoke warmth and friendliness. We like to get a chunky feeling in detail— a solidity.

For a humane balanced tomorrow we are endeavouring to play our part as a member of a collective leadership, alongside the economist, politician, sociologist and moralist, looking beyond what has become known as the traditional image of the architect.

St John's Village, Glebe, NSW
Shopping Centre, Bankstown, NSW

Bankstown Square Shopping Centre
Bankstown, NSW

A building like this takes time to be accepted as part of the established scene—a populous suburban community—time to be understood and appreciated. As it is used, it will become a natural part of the life of the local people. It will be moulded by their needs, their tastes, their interests; be mellowed with time like the market place.

This centre, really a complex of build-ings, is essentially a simple backdrop to the activities for which it is intended. It encloses some 680,000 sq.ft, having all servicing completely separated from the shopper, providing two ground levels with the opportunity for people to pass by every shop in one, two-level, circular movement. Parking is provided for 2,500 cars on decked roof and landscaped levels.

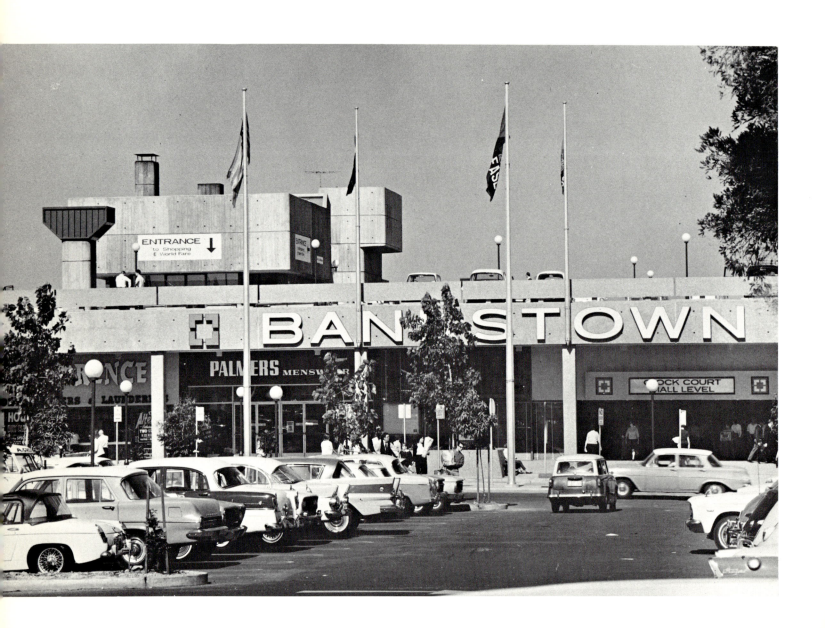

Shopping Centre, Bankstown, NSW

to Shops ➡

Shopping Centre, Bankstown, NSW

St John's Village
Glebe, NSW

A simple brick and tile cluster of individual homes from home for the aged,
located in an inner urban setting and
in contact with a fine stone church.

Here with a density of 100 persons an
acre, privacy and a sense of community are allowed to co-exist.

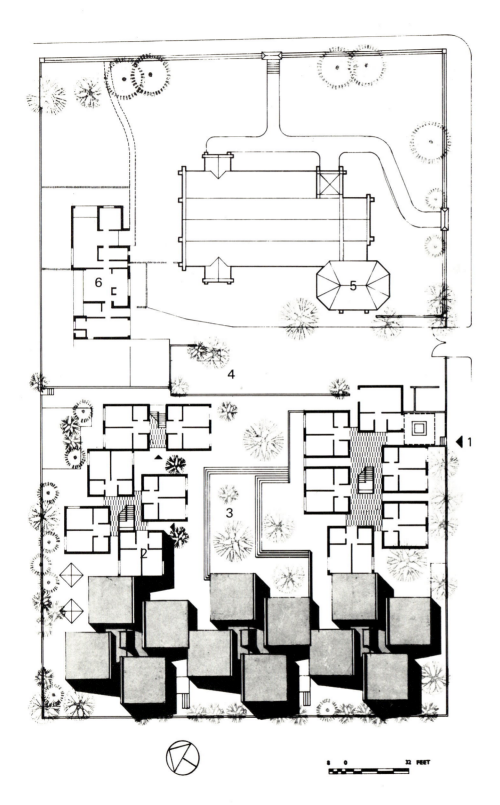

1 entry
2 cluster of 2-storey blocks
3 courtyard
4 parking
5 existing church and grounds
6 rectory

The client thought the buildings had something Mediterranean about them; one tenant, an ex-missionary, was reminded of buildings she had known in Japan; another tenant thanked us for allowing her a small share in our hopes and aspiration for a relaxed yet sensitive home for folk in their latter years. One and all loved the Village, rich and poor, young and old, educated and simple. An architect friend summed it up—'It is understandable to the man in the street, because it is what it is; and the ordinary person sees that a door is a door, a roof is a roof, a wall is a wall'. The individual element, though not commonplace, is readily recognizable; the whole is then recognizable and acceptable. These buildings have helped to re-establish that vital rapport between architect and people—ordinary people.

St John's Village, Glebe, NSW

St John's Village, Glebe, NSW

The environs of Melbourne are mainly flat, and offer few reasonable characteristics for outward environment— physical forms of urban living are set into a rigid pattern of development, of standard subdivisions of approximately eight to an acre (50' 0" x 140' 0").

'Inside-out' architecture permits better control of the environmental aspects of the design, and privacy and change of scene are readily achieved, giving the architect more scope for design control. Through providing inside environmental control, rather than relying upon outside chaos, a form of architecture develops, of discovery and surprise, which, we hope, will relieve the inhabitants of the tensional bond with twentieth century world outside. Planning forms the key to pleasant family living, multi-use of spaces and adjustment to changing user requirements. We aim at a more rational approach to related physical and functional use of spaces, producing great spatial scale within a restricted building size.

The architectural character is produced through two major considerations imposed on architecture by a changing and, in some ways, culturally immature society. Means and taste are generally somewhat restricted, producing a state of architectural 'caution' or understatement, and we thus provide a simple, basic form of building, allowing for cost control, taste control and, sometimes, limited building skills. Although taste, being individual, is uncontrollable, our tendency towards architectural over-simplification will allow personal taste in interior elements to unite with the building, rather than conflict with it.

Architectural discipline is required to permit public taste to grow through discovery rather than through dogma. We are hopeful that this control may lead to the development of a regional character and perhaps increase the number of patrons of architecture, both on a large and a small scale.

Speculative Town House, South Yarra, Vic

Speculative Town House, South Yarra, Vic

Speculative Town House
South Yarra, Vic

On a site one mile from city centre, the programme was to incorporate a new dwelling attached to rear of existing dwelling, thus providing two separate houses.

The new house had to be designed within a restricted area, and existing trees and shrubs were retained. Privacy and controlled orientation were aimed for, plus a simple character, permitting the purchaser the opportunity of expressing his own taste. The construction is of timber floor and roof, with brick walls.

Ten Flat Units
Toorak, Vic

The client required a variety of accommodation in an existing residential area with building height restriction of two storeys.

The architects have produced five two-bedroomed units with private court-yard gardens on the ground floor and five three-bedroomed units with patio balconies at first floor level.

The convenience of undercover car parking with direct access to each flat has been provided, giving protection from the weather, convenient delivery of goods etc.

Construction is of brick, with reinforced concrete floors and stairs and metal deck roof.

Twelve Studio Flats
South Yarra, Vic

This scheme is unusual in that the flats
are of a two-storeyed type. Car parking
is located under the building at lower
ground floor level.

The flats are designed with an environment created by incorporating a patio
within each flat, for private external
living. The patios are approximately
12' 0'' x 7' 0''.

Internal finishes are painted bagged
brick walls, timber ceilings and concealed lighting to produce an intimate
character and an atmosphere in tune
with inner suburban living.

Eight Town Houses
South Yarra, Vic

The client required a group of town houses on a site one and a half miles from the GPO, two minutes from the tram and opposite a park.

The concept offers a unique form of urban living, whereby each house has its own private garden environment.

Each house has a living room, dining room, kitchen and guest toilet on the ground floor, and, on the first floor, a large double bedroom, second double bedroom, bathroom and laundry. The lower ground floor provides under-cover parking and storage space.

Materials used were natural oiled redwood for all windows and ceilings, and 4'' square quarry tiles on the floors of kitchens and toilets. The finishes used achieved a character not normally found in general speculative development.

Healy House
Ocean Grove, Vic

The client required a residence to provide permanent accommodation for grandmother and holiday accommodation for son, wife and two children. The most important ancillary requirement was that a 360° view of the sea and inland bushland should be possible.

The house is conceived in three levels to obtain view and to suit planning requirements. A bolted timber column and exposed beam construction was used to effect rapid erection and economy through standardization. The whole structure, plus wall joinery system and floor, was pre-cut and drilled before delivery to site.

All exposed timber and joinery has been treated with 'Timba-ol' stain to obtain a brown-black colour. Exposed solid walls are painted white. All infill panels are of hardboard and asbestos cement painted white.

Roofing is pressed metal tray deck, 24-gauge, with downpipes flush with external columns.

Grandstand for the
Perak Turf Club
Ipoh, Malaysia

The grandstand, to accommodate 6,000 people, is the major element in a complex of buildings which won an international competition in 1964. Malaysia's hot, humid climate requires special provision for cross-ventilation and sun control. In the grandstand, air-conditioning is provided to VIP areas and mechanical ventilation to spectator areas.

The two spectator functions of viewing and betting are linked with a wide concourse running the full length of the grandstand at all levels. Contained within this artery are the main vertical circulation systems (stairs, escalators), also other service facilities, and lifts to VIP boxes, press, radio, stewards, photo finish and judges' tower. The type of construction used throughout the scheme is related to the local economy, and the availability of materials. The main structure of the grandstand is of reinforced concrete, either pre-stressed or post-tensioned. The main frames consist of two hollow service columns supporting balanced cantilever beams. Roof and intermediate floors are made up of U-shaped pre-cast concrete planks spanning between main frames.

Materials generally are used with a natural finish, and selected Malaysian timbers have been used for all joinery and furniture.

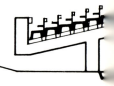

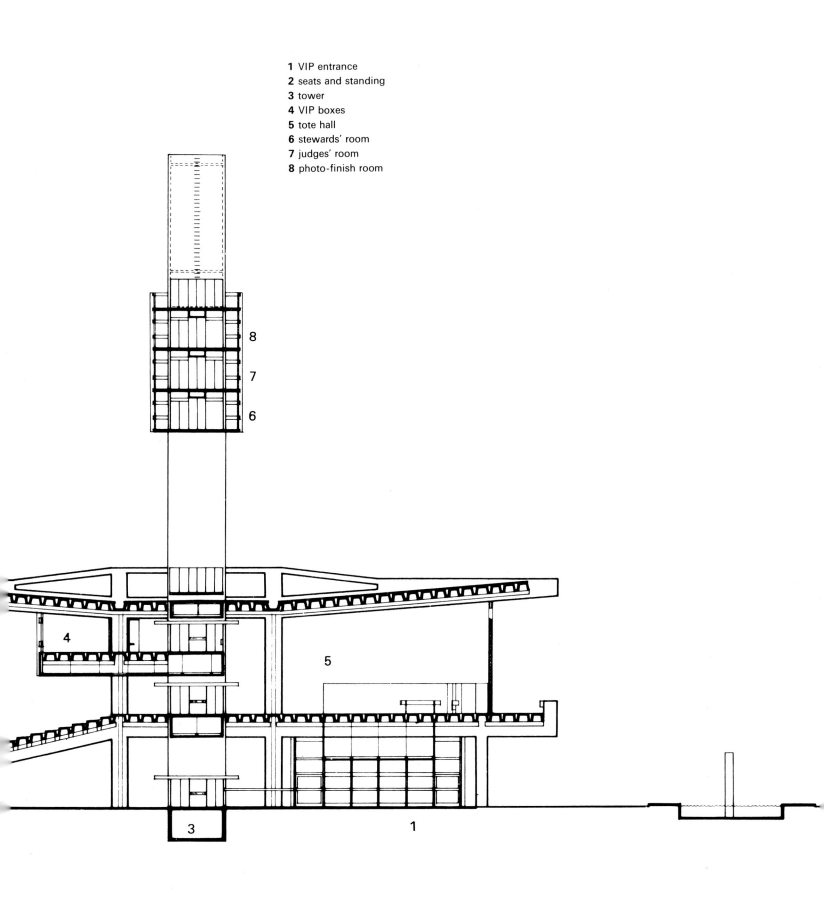

1 VIP entrance
2 seats and standing
3 tower
4 VIP boxes
5 tote hall
6 stewards' room
7 judges' room
8 photo-finish room

8

7

6

4

5

3

1

Partners: Stanley Smith, Peter Johnson, Tom Heath, Peter Keys.

A building is a shelter for certain activities. But activities change with time; often, these days, with very little time. Some changes are predictable, others by their nature are not. The building must be as flexible as can be afforded, robust enough in conception to endure change.

In Sydney, where most of our work is, the building has to give shelter from the heaviest rainfall of any major city, 70 mph winds, big city noise, hot summer sun and glaring sky. Massive internal walls and floors flatten the peaks of the diurnal temperature range and reduce sound transmission. Deep overhangs cut the glare and the sun, and help to keep out the rain, even at the expense of permanent lighting of work areas. The sun is kind to strong modelling, cruel to the bland or finicky. In a rapidly developing country, there is never enough capital. The budget must be met—or cut. Brick, timber, tiles and concrete are cheap if you accept traditional craft methods. When you have to build a skyscraper on a confined site in a short time traditional methods won't do, so the Sydney Water Board building for example is made largely of pre-cast concrete; floors, stairs and walls were made elsewhere and hung on the frame.

Finally, teamwork. The plans for most buildings are too complicated for any one man to carry about in his head. If a team is to design a building everything must be made explicit and, if necessary, debated. This is not easy; care and thought must be given to the techniques of teamwork if the result is to be architecture. But in many cases it is teamwork or chaos.

Water Board Building, Sydney, NSW
University of NSW

Extensions to the Main Building
University of NSW,
Kensington, NSW

This building provides additional space for the School of Architecture and Building and is itself capable of extension to an additional two floors. It is reinforced concrete framed, directly linked to the first building erected on the site, and consists of two wings which accommodate laboratories, studios and offices.

Because of the nature of the site one main façade faces north and, to exclude sun at all times from the studios, a system of concrete hoods and adjustable timber louvres has been provided. To maintain lighting levels in the studios, permanent supplementary artificial lighting is installed.

The studios are divided by sliding red cedar doors so that teaching environments of different scales can be created. These screens provide large pin-up areas, and there are also pin-up panels in the corridors suitable for exhibitions and criticism.

Head Office Extensions for
The Metropolitan Water, Sewerage
and Drainage Board
Sydney, NSW

The exterior of the building is a direct expression of its plan elements which are defined by the structure, and the sun control and cladding systems. Service cores at the eastern and western ends provide an effective barrier against heat gain from the sun and the precast concrete sun visors on the northern face control sun penetration in order to reduce solar radiation, thus reducing initial and running costs of the airconditioning system and controlling sky glare, as well as serving as external window cleaning platforms.

The structure is a steel frame, with the general office area supported by three rigid frames spaced at 23' 0" centres and spanning a width of 73' 0". Floors are constructed in precast pretensioned twin 'T' concrete units.

Water Board Building, Sydney, NSW

Water Board Building, Sydney, NSW

House for Professor Peter Johnson
Chatswood, NSW

The house is built on the side of a typical wooded gully of Sydney's North Shore. The rocky site is covered with native trees and shrubs and has been left in its natural state.

The materials of the house have been selected to be in sympathy with the character of the site. Walls are clinker bricks left bare, with raked joints inside and out; windows, timber oil-stained black; ceilings, Monterey Pine; cupboards, doors and door frames, polished Mountain Ash; floor generally Tallowwood with red quarry tiles in the entrance, dining and kitchen areas.

The house has five levels which accommodate to the levels of the site, taking advantage of bush views, getting good orientation and placing rooms and windows so that they will receive cooling winds in the summer. Each level houses a different group of activities; the staircase becomes the core of the house. Careful consideration was given to sun control, thus there are balconies on the north and a minimum of western windows.

Johnson House, Chatswood, NSW

The practice of architecture now has been rendered far more exacting than at any previous time. Apart from the tremendous increase in scale and volume of work, we are faced with the problems of an impersonal, corporate client, an unprecedented expansion in technological knowledge and ability, and a rapid and accelerating rate of social and economic change.

It has become increasingly difficult for anyone to comprehend all the factors which impinge on the evolution of environment, and yet this is what an architect must do in order to make any worthwhile contribution to that evolution. It is environment we are concerned with, after all—not the creation of single monuments, but the creation of a stimulating, manageable environment which will support man's activities, increase his awareness of his world, and yet be within his economic limitations and remain so for a considerable period.

We have the technical ability to do this now, but it requires the removal of the architect from his traditional position as an 'artist creator' to a new role as a co-ordinator, technician and organizer with a creative vision of an end result which somehow transcends such things. This is no contradiction, for to properly satisfy any environmental problem the architect has to be acutely aware of the things which move the spirit of man, as well as the more tangible, rational, definable things. He has, most importantly, to create something which will, as actively and accurately as possible, satisfy the physical, economic, climatic controls of the brief, but that will be nothing unless his creation is so moulded and fitting to its place that it improves the environment by its existence, expresses its purpose clearly and beautifully, and is a product of its time, not an eclectic repetition of some age past. If it does these things it will be a genuine and worthwhile piece of architecture.

Presbyterian Agricultural College, Paterson, NSW

C. B. Alexander
Presbyterian Agricultural College
Paterson, NSW

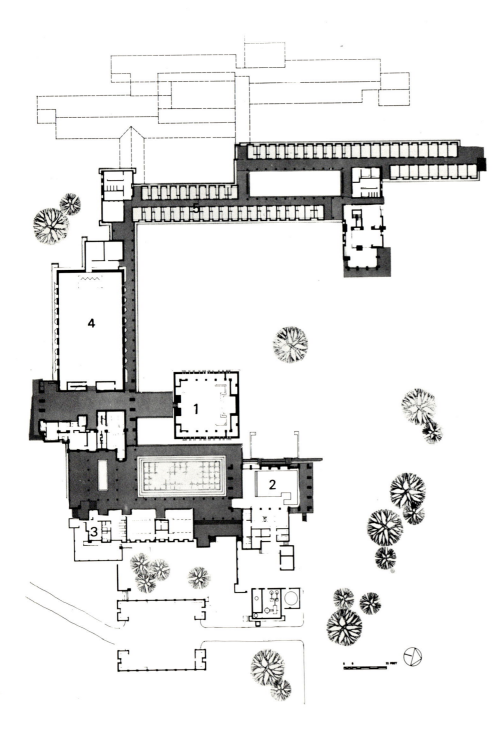

In accommodating 120 boys, with
common room, classrooms, assembly
hall, library, administrative offices, etc.,
we wanted to create a collegiate
atmosphere with a strong sense of
community. We therefore grouped the
buildings in long horizontal wings
around an open-ended court facing
north and the magnificent views over
the Paterson River. The chapel is the
free standing pivot of the arrangement.
We were able to draw on an adequate
labour force from the nearby centres of
population, and so used locally made
bricks and tiles, and locally milled
timbers.

1 chapel
2 dining
3 administration
4 hall
5 single bedrooms

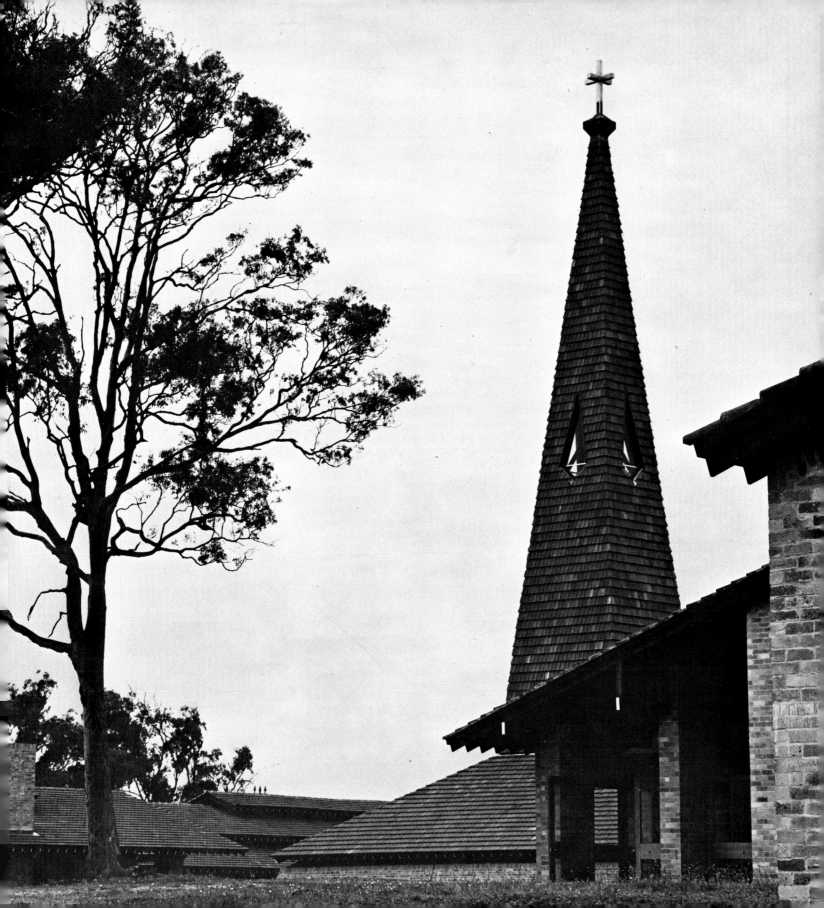

Presbyterian Agricultural College, Paterson, NSW

St Andrew's
Presbyterian Boys' Home
Leppington, NSW

Our research showed that delinquency
derives largely from some sort of social
rejection and we wanted this building
to help the rehabilitation of the boys.
We emphasized a sense of ownership
and belonging by giving each boy a
completely distinct area over which he
could have complete control. The
economic and psychological problems
inherent in single rooms had to be
avoided, so we planned the 3-boy
units in a 'T', with each boy having one
wing. We used simple, maintenance-
free materials in a loose attenuated
plan form.

Presbyterian Church
Manilla, NSW

This small church, in north-west NSW, had the dual problem of a very tight budget and a site on the black soil plains which was liable to 2" differential movement. The church is consequently light and flexible, and we developed a system of off-site prefabricated, stressed skin, plywood trusses previously used in a house. The trusses were flexibly joined by ply panels, top chord to bottom chord, and taken off a reinforced concrete beam, which put the ground slab into constant tension, thus minimizing the effect of movement and reducing costs very substantially. The tiling battens act as lateral ties.

The three buildings illustrated are a very small part of the output of one of the largest architectural offices in Australia. The Government Architect for New South Wales is responsible for the public building programme in a rapidly expanding State with a population approaching five million people. Over 120 qualified architects are employed on a programme of buildings for health, education, police and justice, welfare, offices and other fields.

As with any very large office designing a great variety of buildings to be located in areas having extreme variations in geographical and climatic conditions, and in the building materials available, there are not always characteristics common to all buildings. A policy of delegation of work to specialized sections and to individual project architects gives further scope for a variety of approaches.

Public buildings must nevertheless be designed having in mind somewhat different criteria to those applying to many commercial and private structures; in particular a relatively long life span, durable and maintenance-free construction and finishes, and limited, well-defined cost targets.

These and other factors have tended to produce, amongst the best work of the office, an architecture which is direct and logical in use of materials, aiming at a simple and economical solution to each set of problems. Where possible, applied finishes are avoided in favour of direct expression of primary and structural materials.

During the last ten years the small but steady flow of staff to and from Europe and North America for the purpose of advanced academic study or for investigation of specific building types, has both overcome any sense of isolation which may have been characteristic in the past, and helped to keep the office informed of international architectural developments.

If an architecture characteristic of the Government Architect's office has evolved, it has been not as the result of centrally formulated policy, but as a logical response to the complex and particular problems of designing public buildings for the State.

NSW State Government Offices, Sydney, NSW

NSW State Government Offices
Sydney, NSW

This building houses a number of Departments of the New South Wales Government.

The State Premier's Office and Department occupy part of the prestige office and reception accommodation in the 9-storey block to the east, while the 8-storey office block to the north contains general office space, a staff cafeteria and an auditorium.

The 34-storey tower, which is interconnected with the two other wings, consists of a concrete lift and service core with radiating steel floor beams carrying structural steel floors topped with concrete and fireproof sprayed to the soffits, supported at the perimeter by composite steel and concrete columns.

The building is designed to a module of 4' 8" with a 2" construction module resulting in a greatly simplified detailing.

External columns are sheeted with black bronze cladding. Black bronze is also used for the window frames which are fitted with anti-glare glass set in neoprene gaskets. Reconstructed stone panels are used as solid walls where they are required and as cladding for the perimeter beams.

Secondary School
Ryde, NSW

This school was designed to be built in stages to accommodate 1,000 children between the ages of 10 and 18 years, and to offer a full range of academic and manual arts subjects.

The five-acre site is only about one third the area normally allocated for a school of this size, and the steep slope added a further complication. The problem was overcome by using a split-level design, the first for a school building in NSW, and utilizing the slope to form, on three levels, a series of stepping interlocking quadrangles enclosed by classrooms.

The belltower, serving as a focal point and rostrum in the central assembly area, is designed to house also the incinerator stack and switch room. Existing gum trees on the site were preserved as far as possible and incorporated into the layout of buildings and courtyards.

Construction is steel frame, painted brown where exposed, with cream brick infill walls. Exterior timbers are oiled, rough-sawn western red cedar. Dark-olive roofing tiles were specially chosen to blend with the colour of surrounding bush. Concrete paving was brushed to expose the aggregate. Internal finishes are: walls, 6'' Mountain Ash planks, fixed horizontally with ship-lapped joints; ceilings, sprayed vermiculite to lower floor, Gyprock to upper floor; floors, vinyl tiles on concrete slab.

Secondary School, Ryde, NSW

Secondary School, Ryde, NSW

Mona Vale District Hospital
Mona Vale, NSW

A new hospital to provide for an initial 150 patients and capable of expansion to 250 beds in the future. Accommodation was required for out-patients, casualty, X-ray, pathology, medical, surgical, obstetrics, gynaecology and associated quarters for nurses and medical officers.

The structure is a bolted steel frame, with metal deck flooring. External walls are white face brick with aluminium window frames.

Mona Vale District Hospital, Mona Vale, NSW

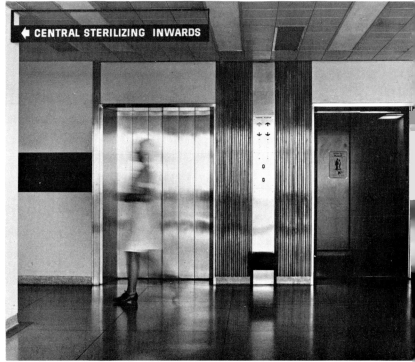

It should go without saying that every building must represent as far as possible a perfect answer to practical problems. The means employed must be the most appropriate economic-structural for the solution, gaining the maximum with minimum of labour content. Let the will of the building needs, the will of our level of industrialization, and of our climate, be done. Unless we give these truthful form, the building will wither of rejection and the discomfort and unhappiness of its users. But even all this can be worthless unless it is brought to life by the designer's firmly based and valid aesthetic intentions.

And can one say what these should be? In modern architecture there are definite and generally discernible aesthetic criteria which any designer can abandon only at his peril: *Space:* Our eyes thrill to an architecture of space (in contrast to the solid volume and form of most traditional building) — it is its language of the intimate and simultaneously infinite, the life-giving elements and subtleties of light and shade. *Structure:* We succumb to the skilled defying of gravity which has been in other ways the aspiration of man throughout history. Not structural acrobatics, but structure revealing its logical form — to clearly see and feel it take stress and to understand the simple direct way in which it was physically achieved. *Visual opposition:*

Opposition will give life to environment. Not all transparency and not all solidity, not all soft and not all hard, but a skilled visual interplay between opposites. Planes opposing each other in space, verticals against horizontals, solid against void, cold colour against warm, curve against straight line and above all in Australia's climate, sunlight against shade.

It can only be through understanding, through education, that the true ethic of architecture will be recognized. Only by sincere and humble understanding can an end be put to the unruly ill-mannered building excess of today so that our buildings will have integrity and will truly be part of our time and place.

*Blues Point Towers and
Australia Square, Sydney, NSW*

House
Turramurra, NSW

The property is on a slope and looks north toward a magnificent view of virgin bushland.

The ample ground, and a desire to avoid a single outlook only, resulted in a building which is freely exposed on all sides so that varying views become part of the interior.

A rectangular mass of building is hollowed by an open centre, with a well piercing it vertically to admit sunlight to an open play space below.

From the rigid rectangle of the structure, 'tentacles' reach out and anchor it to the surrounding land: the stone retaining walls, the ramp and the louvre fence.

Australia Square
Sydney, NSW

The design concept of Australia Square aims to solve the problem of urban redevelopment in a comprehensive way. Present-day town planning tends to be haphazard; generally, old buildings of three or four storeys are replaced by new ones several times their size and occupying their entire site. These buildings are often robbed of air and light as the sites around them become more and more congested.

Over thirty properties were amalgamated to create this large site of approximately one and a half acres. Instead of covering the whole area with a 12-storey building (which is the regulated limit of floor space), two structures were built—a 13-storey block and a 50-storey, 560 ft. high tower, covering only twenty-five percent of the site.

The tower building, by use of a circular form, brings a new openness into the congested heart of Sydney. The shape is an ideal structural form for tall buildings resisting wind loads. By consulting Professor Pier Luigi Vervi, the world authority in concrete design, the project gained logical, economic and significant aesthetic form in the design of the curved, ribbed ferro cement floor system and the tapered exterior columns.

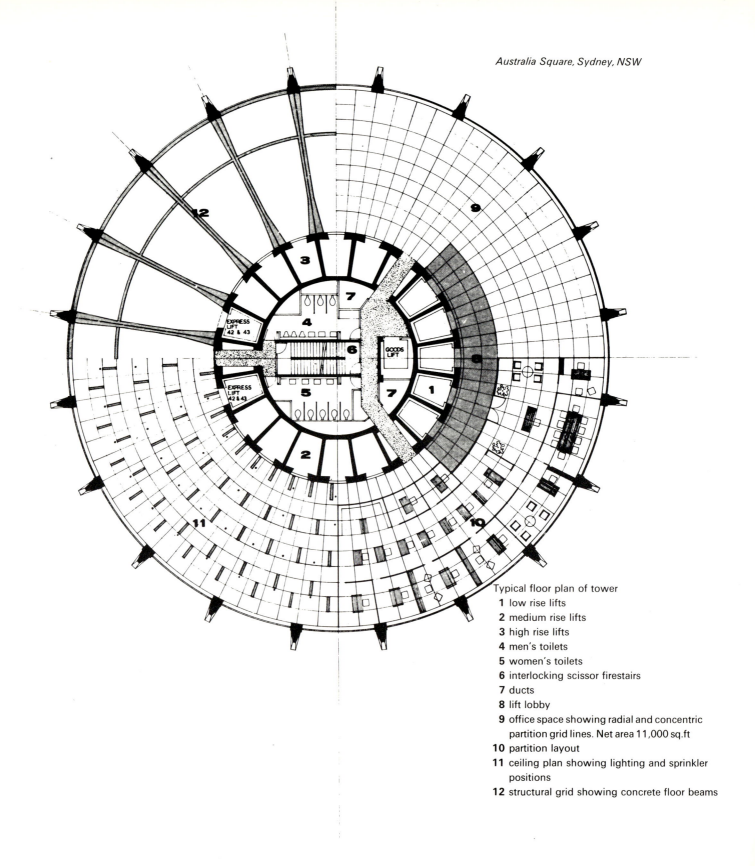

Australia Square, Sydney, NSW

Typical floor plan of tower
1 low rise lifts
2 medium rise lifts
3 high rise lifts
4 men's toilets
5 women's toilets
6 interlocking scissor firestairs
7 ducts
8 lift lobby
9 office space showing radial and concentric partition grid lines. Net area 11,000 sq.ft
10 partition layout
11 ceiling plan showing lighting and sprinkler positions
12 structural grid showing concrete floor beams

Australia Square, Sydney, NSW

Australia Square, Sydney, NSW

House for Harry Seidler
Killara, NSW

When an architect and his wife, who is also an architect, set out to build their own house for the first time, the choice of site and location is as telling of their attitudes as is the design of the house itself.

This site is inland only eight miles from the city centre of Sydney. It is a broken, ruggedly sloping area cut by large rock ledges and overshadowed by huge eucalyptus trees. This provided scope for 'vertical' dimension, not only in the siting and approach of the house, but also in the interior, due to the resulting multi-level design following the contours.

The main aesthetic aim of the house is not only to have horizontal freedom of space but also, by fusing and opening the various levels into each other and by 'pulling them apart', to create a 2½-storey high open shaft between them, to add a vertical interplay of space.

There are glimpses of through views from the different levels giving always a sense of the areas beyond without any blunt openness of planning. The structural piers, the fireplace and the concrete parapets define these through spaces.

All materials used inside and out are left in their natural state. Their textures emphasize contrast: white against dark grey and primary colours, soft rugs against rugged concrete etc.

Seidler house, Killara, NSW

Seidler house, Killara, NSW

Seidler house, Killara, NSW

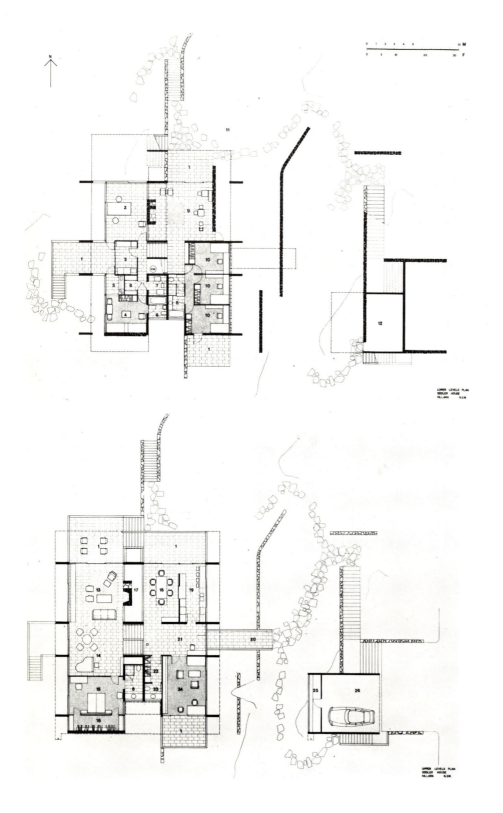

Seidler house, Killara, NSW

1 terrace
2 studio
3 laundry
4 housekeeper's apartment
5 kitchenette
6 cellar
7 air conditioning equipment
8 bathroom
9 children's playroom
10 children's bedrooms
11 garden
12 gardening tools and store
13 living room
14 music room
15 master bedroom
16 dressing room
17 void
18 dining room
19 kitchen
20 entrance bridge
21 entrance gallery
22 coat room
23 wash room
24 library-study
25 workshop
26 garage

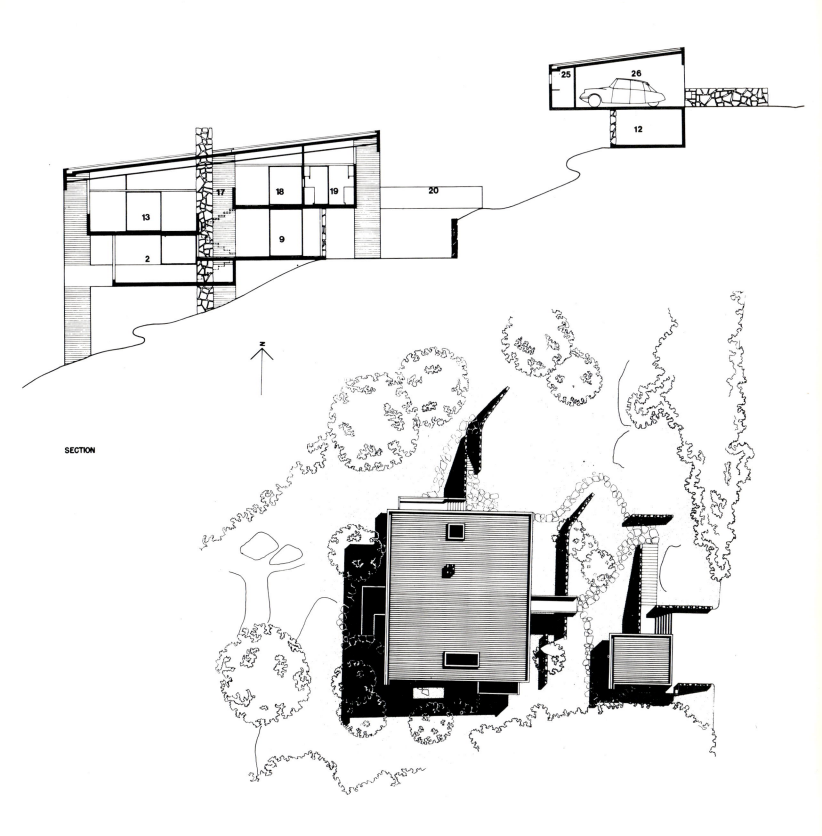

SECTION

N

Seidler house, Killara, NSW

Architectural practices must always recognize the essential characteristics of their times. The pre-eminent patron of today is the corporate client; the economic bias he exerts is as powerful a design influence as are the advances of modern building science. Increasingly, the architect must gear his organization to facilitate communication with large organizations, to understand the economic forces that regulate their building activities and equate them to advanced design and building techniques.

The corporate client has engaged the activities of Yuncken Freeman Architects since its formation in 1933. Starting with hospitals and other institutional commissions, the practice has expanded to serve a wide range of civic, educational, industrial and commercial clients.

In recent years, office buildings have played a major part in the firm's work. Such projects, with their hard-core requirements of economic efficiency and internal flexibility, call for an intensely disciplined design attitude if 'architecture' is to emerge. The structural system must be both the basis and the strength of the design concept; but the designer's concern must not stop with the building alone—it should extend to the building in the context of its total environment. This leads naturally to a strong interest in urban design,

as illustrated in projects such as master planning of La Trobe University and the Civic Centre projects in Canberra.

By concentrating on the essential aspects of architecture, the firm has been able to make some contribution to the advancement of construction techniques. The Royal Insurance Group Building and the State Government Offices are advanced examples, in an evolutionary series of essays, in which the use of precast concrete has been progressively refined. In contrast, the Sidney Myer Music Bowl provides a unique solution to a unique problem, yet shares with the office buildings the same dedication to a structural discipline.

If these buildings have achieved individual quality, it is not from a conscious desire to be different. It is rather from a desire to produce buildings that are vitally of the present, in which today's scientific and technological advances are applied with the clarity and logic of classical principles of design.

Scottish Amicable House, Melbourne, Vic

Scottish Amicable House
Melbourne, Vic

Completed in 1965, this was originally
an investment building. The concrete
frame is clad on both east and west
façades with precast concrete window
units providing sun protection.

State Government Offices Complex
Melbourne, Vic

First prize in an architectural competition to select a design for the new
State Government Offices, Treasury
Place Melbourne. The buildings are
designed to provide first class standard
of office accommodation as well as
not affecting the Victorian period architecture of the associated buildings in
the Government Reserve. The buildings
are reinforced concrete with precast
structural mullions of an exposed
aggregate finish similar to the existing
sandstone buildings nearby. The re-
organization of the area surrounding
these buildings will finally combine
the Treasury Place Gardens to the
south, the State Square and the major
buildings in the area, and the State
Houses of Parliament.

Royal Insurance Group Building
Melbourne, Vic

Completed in 1965 and awarded the
Victorian Architectural Medal in 1967.
The external cladding is pre-glazed
polished black reconstructed granite
precast concrete panels. Each panel is
4' 6" x 12' 0" high, weighing 1½ tons.

Royal Insurance Group Building,
Melbourne, Vic

In 1957 Joern Utzon, the Danish architect, won an international competition for the design of the Sydney Opera House.

'In the Sydney Opera House scheme the idea has been to let the platform cut through like a knife and separate primary and secondary functions completely. On top of the platform the spectators receive the completed work of art and beneath the platform every preparation for it takes place. To express the platform and avoid destroying it is a very important thing, when you start building on top of it. A flat roof does not express the flatness of the platform.

'You can see roofs, curved forms, hanging higher or lower over the plateau. The contrast of forms and the constantly changing heights between these two elements result in spaces of great architectural force made possible by the modern structural approach to concrete construction, which has given so many beautiful tools into the hands of the architect.

'The Sydney Opera House is one of those buildings where the roof is of major importance. It is a house which is completely exposed. The Sydney Opera House is a house which one will see from above, will sail around— because it sits on a point sticking out into a harbour, a very beautiful harbour, a fjord with a lot of inlets. This point is in the middle of the city and the city rises on both sides of the fjord so the Opera House is a focal point. This means that one could not design a building for such an exposed position without paying attention to the roof. One could not have a flat roof filled with ventilation pipes—in fact, one must have a fifth façade which is just as important as the other façades. Furthermore, people will sail around it, there are ferries sailing past and large ships coming in—the big harbour is just outside and the large bridge nearby, so people will see it as a round thing. They will not see it as a house in a street, either along the street or across.'

Extracts from *Zodiac* 10 and 14.

Opera House, Sydney, NSW   **Vision** - *original sketch by Joern Utzon*

SHELL A2

SHELL A3

SHELL A4

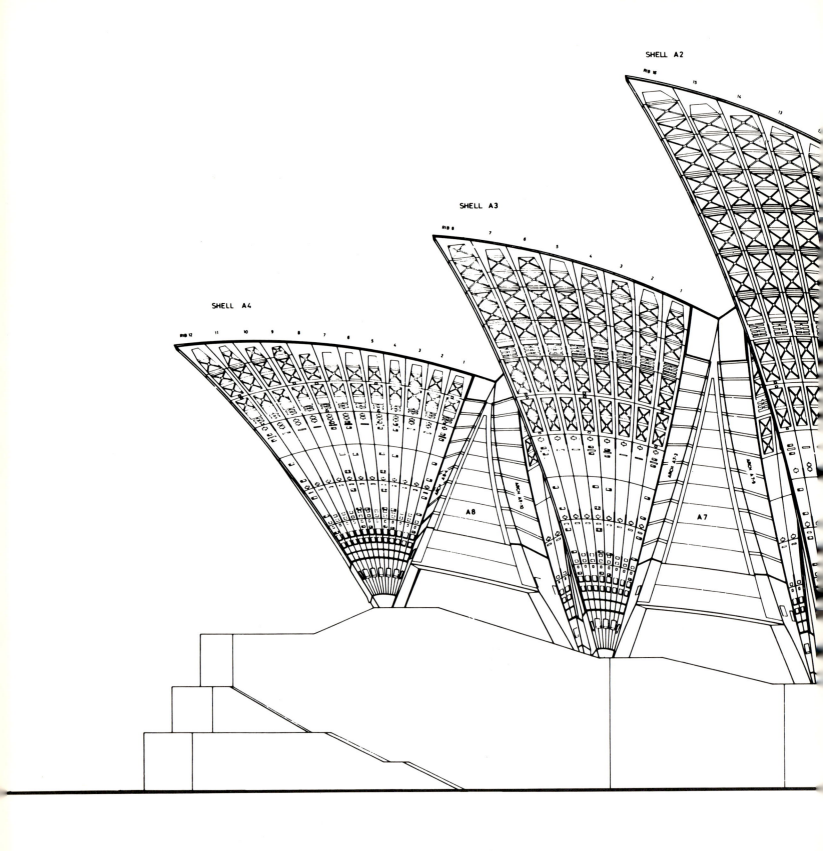

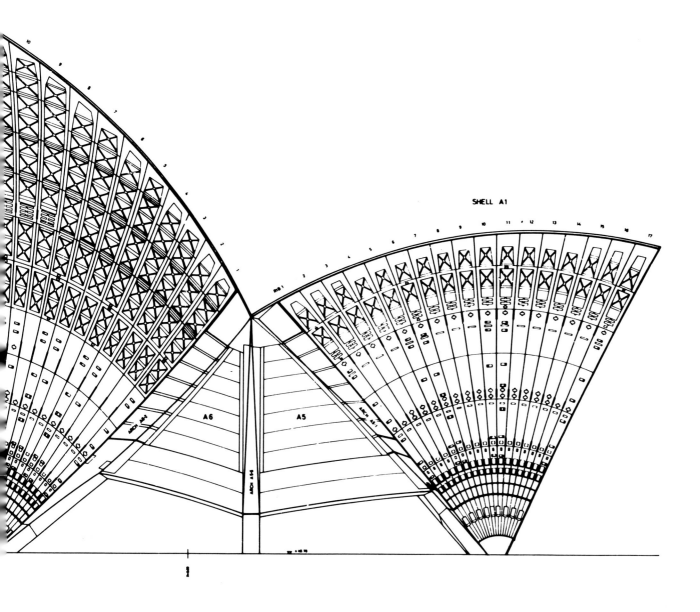

SHELL A1

A6   A5

Opera House, Sydney, NSW   **Fact** - *working drawing by Ove Arup & Partners*

Opera House, Sydney, NSW **Reality**

'In a technological world it is all too easy to present man's wonders and achievements as ends in themselves, forgetting that behind these achievements are people who make them possible, and the wider community they serve. The concept, design and construction of the Sydney Opera House stand as an affirmation for twentieth century man—that by his imagination and by his own hand he can shape his world to his needs.'

Ove Arup

Ove Arup & Partners
Consulting Engineers
Opera House
Sydney, NSW